T0305378

An Alternative Approach to Family Business

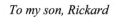

To my son, Rickard

An Alternative Approach to Family Business

A Theory of Socio-Material Weaving

Mona Ericson

Professor Emerita of Strategy and Organization and CeFEO Affiliated Professor, Jönköping International Business School, Sweden

Cheltenham, UK • Northampton, MA, USA

Cover Image: Engin Akyurt on Unsplash.

Published by
Edward Elgar Publishing Limited
The Lypiatts
15 Lansdown Road
Cheltenham
Glos GL50 2JA
UK

Edward Elgar Publishing, Inc.
William Pratt House
9 Dewey Court
Northampton
Massachusetts 01060
USA

A catalogue record for this book
is available from the British Library

Library of Congress Control Number: 2021945050

This book is available electronically in the **Elgar**online
Business subject collection
http://dx.doi.org/10.4337/9781800379077

ISBN 978 1 80037 906 0 (cased)
ISBN 978 1 80037 907 7 (eBook)

Printed and bound by CPI Group (UK) Ltd, Croydon, CR0 4YY

Contents

Acknowledgements

Tällberg is a small village beautifully located on the slope down to Lake Siljan in Dalarna, Sweden. Extending between geography and philosophy it opens a world of interesting people and stories that allow insights into the social and the material. Many thanks go to Signe Alm, Margareta Aspman, Mats Blomqvist, Hans Erik Börjeson, Olof Alm Keys, Staffan Malmqvist, Anders Sandberg, Inger Sandberg, Per Sandberg, Kerstin Sanfridson, Fredrik Svedberg, Anders Åkerblad, Carina Åkerblad, Christina Åkerblad, Elias Granat Åkerblad, Gunilla Åkerblad, Jerk Åkerblad, Lovisa Åkerblad, and Rosanna Åkerblad for their valuable contributions to this socio-material book.

I also wish to thank the President and the Vice President of the local heritage society in Tällberg, hotel receptionists and artists for providing me with interesting information about Tällberg, the hotels and artworks.

I owe a special thanks to CeFEO, Centre for Family Entrepreneurship and Ownership, at Jönköping International Business School, and my research colleagues. I greatly appreciate being a CeFEO affiliated Professor.

Finally, I wish to thank Magnus Bergvalls Stiftelse for their financial support that allowed me to make multiple visits to Tällberg and carry out the study.

1. Under the name of Tällberg

There will never be the same, always new days and lights. On a summer day everything is blue, the lake, the sky – a blue dreamland with white glitter in all this blue, white clouds, white geese on the lake and a white steamer gliding over the blue surface, white birch trees like straight shining candles ...

(Forslund, 1922, p. 37)[1]

These words convey impressions that are colourfully put together under the name of 'Tällberg', which on a map drawn according to cartographic conventions appears as a Swedish village. When reading the words of Forslund (1922) we are compelled to an interpretation and understanding that give association to an impressionistic painting. We become attuned to the narrator's sense of the shifting blue with white weft threads going through materials that relate us to the sky, earth and water. With reference to Tällberg other materials also get our attention, in various ways colouring inhabitants' descriptions of business activities, constituted of the sociality of human interactions and relations. The descriptions are mediated narratively in the form of stories that help advancing our understanding of family business as an emergent phenomenon. 'Family business' dissolves into activities with which people are entwined, immersed in materials spatially extended.

In complement to existing family business research the book suggests an alternative approach, a theory of socio-material weaving that purports narrative information in the form of stories to be conducive to an understanding of family business *as activities* engaged with materials related to spatiality. The theory development process is stimulated by Tällberg place materials and a problematization that highlights the need to add to existing family business research a spatial-material dimension with a concern for the hermeneutic-phenomenological idea that we are beings-in-the-world, intimately involved *with* the world *with* others *with* materials. As pointed out in the book, the social gains considerable attention from family business scholars with little discussion of the spatial material.

Since the notion of place is closely related to space, the theory is also concerned with space, clearly differentiating between space and place.

The 'weaving' activity included in the suggested theory implies bringing together the sociality of activities with the material, illustrating that materials are appropriated in activities in the promotion of existential space, and experientially explored in a bodily lived sense in relation to place. Informed by the philosophical tradition of hermeneutic phenomenology a theory of socio-material weaving presumes interpretation and understanding, occurring as stories evolve in between the storytellers and the researcher, interlaced with insights drawn from existing theories of family business, social and material, space and place. Tentative in character, the theory aims for plausibility, rather than testability, validity and generalizability, laying out lines that can be followed in subsequent theory construction (cf. Stewart et al., 2010; Weick, 1989).

The family business is everywhere. Family business constitutes one of the fastest growing research areas today. Students and scholars from all over the world study the topic of family business. An approach that theorizes family business as socio-material weaving could inspire interpretation and understanding that extend beyond a view that insists on conceiving of family business as a predefined context that relates to the wider context of an external environment. In terms of 'good theory' it aims for newness and usefulness (Shephard & Suddaby, 2017; Weick, 1989), opening up avenues of research that bring together the social and the material in an account of a spatial-related material dimension. It draws on stories that tell about people's entwinement with a variety of business activities, sorrows encumbered and challenges faced, and these stories could also be of interest to practitioners, providing relevance for 'practice-present and future' (Corley & Gioia, 2011, p. 26) increasing the awareness that activities extend through materials.

STIMULATING THEORY BUILDING

Geographically, Tällberg describes a piece of a Swedish landscape, a spatial expanse labelled 'village'[2] with 200 inhabitants and eight hotels beautifully located on the slope down to Lake Siljan in the province of Dalarna, during the Middle Ages the most populous province in Sweden. Lake Siljan was created 377 million years ago when a meteorite crashed into the earth. A giant lump of space rock formed a ring-shaped crater estimated to have had a diameter of 40 kilometres and a depth of five kilometres (Dalarna, 2016).

Old photos, tourist brochures and books produced by the Tällberg inhabitants themselves render a history that goes back to the mid-1400s when the name *Thaellebaerghe*, which means 'Mountain of Pine Trees', was used. Back then people involved in farming, kept cattle and cultivated a piece of land for their own livelihood. In the early 1900s, the railroad was built, making a larger geographical area accessible. Trails were laid that made it possible for people to travel more than 1200 kilometres, all the way from Stockholm via the village of Tällberg to the town of Kiruna in Lappland, the northernmost province in Sweden. The train was called 'Dollar-train'. With the growing number of tourist arrivals in Tällberg new opportunities for earning money were constructed and as a result, some farmhouses were converted into hotels. The Dollar-train made a stop in Tällberg where buses took the passengers to the hotels. The development of the railroad helped to push farming families into changing their ways of living, gradually decreasing the involvement in farming activities and increasingly engaging in hotel business activities (Tällbergs Byalag, 2007). Activities were also oriented towards guest home lodging and eduction (Alm, 1969).

The book presents five stories that direct attention to business activities in association with hotels, a guest home and a school, constituted of human interactions and relations, interwoven with materials that relate to the Tällberg place and other materials drawn into and used *with* activities. Under the name of Tällberg we catch a glimpse of a dynamic transformative field of material relations where family businesses dissolve into activities.

EXISTING FAMILY BUSINESS RESEARCH: LITTLE CONCERN FOR THE MATERIAL

Family business constitutes one of the fastest growing research areas today with students and scholars from around the world covering a wide range of themes. A review of more than 450 articles published over the past three decades in top journals displays that the six most important themes of family business research are the management of the firm, performance and growth, characteristics and attributes, interpersonal family dynamics, governance, and succession (Evert et al., 2016). The social dimension of family business receives much interest in this research (Chapter 2). Studies incorporate analyses of human interactions and relations, highlighting socioemotional wealth, familiness, stewardship and cultural competence, for example. A material dimension associated with space and place is to a large extent left out from scholarly discussions of the social.

Family business, common derivatives of which are family enterprise, family firm and family company, is most often treated as an open system consisting of family and business reciprocally related to each other (Zahra & Sharma, 2004), figuratively modelled by two intersecting circles (Lansberg, 1983). 'The family system influences the business system through different formal and informal mechanisms', explains Mazzelli (2015, p. 40). Family business signifies 'a type of organization that is intentionally formed as a combination of two otherwise separate social categories' (Whetten et al., 2014, p. 480) and often entails an instrumental use of culture and values (cf. Sorenson, 2014). The extent and nature of the family's involvement in the business are in some studies measured by scaling techniques focused on culture and values (Astrachan et al., 2002; García-Alvarez & López-Sintas, 2001; Klein et al., 2005).

It is argued that the co-evolvement of family and business suggests a 'truly realistic' approach to understanding family business (Neubauer, 2003, p. 269), a realism that also serves as the basis of the three-circle model which comprises the subsystems of family, business and ownership (Gersick et al., 1997; Tagiuri & Davis, 1996) and gives culture the role of an integrating mechanism for the three subsystems (Fletcher et al., 2012). Through what is termed 'bulleye' another subsystem is added, that of management (Pieper & Klein, 2007). The bulleye emphasizes the open system features as regards feedback loops and reciprocal relationships between the subsystems and between the whole system and the external environment (cf. Rautiainen et al., 2012). The family business system is affected by external and internal environmental conditions and depending on the flexibility of the management of this system, a 'fit' is achieved between the external and the internal (cf. Kammerlander et al., 2015). 'The core rational is that flexibility enables adaptability to the changing internal and external environment', assert Sharma and Salvato (2013, p. 37). The family firm is a bounded social entity that interacts with the wider external context (Martinez & Aldrich, 2014).

The family business, accordingly, is attributed an inside and an outside, a description that prioritizes relationships between the subsystems that make up the whole. In line with this prioritizing, the 'components-of-involvement' and the 'essence' definitional approaches differentiate family business as a unique entity readily available for study. The former approach focuses on the family's involvement in ownership, management or governance of the business and on who the family members are, and the latter on behavioural distinctiveness of the family business (Sharma & Salvato, 2013).

Indeed, there are many ways of defining family business. 'Regardless of the family business definition utilized, one consistent issue arises. Family businesses are owned and/or operative by a group of individuals who are family', inform Ring et al. (2017, p. 160). Family business is a business in which a family has a share of ownership and voting rights that allow substantial influence in terms of control and management of the business (Neubauer, 2003).

Apparently the systems view introduces family business as a finalized entity (Helin, 2011) with little attention paid to how the social interweaves with the material with a concern for spatiality.

WITH A CONCERN FOR THE MATERIAL

While family business research has largely disregarded materials, organizational research has shown a growing interest in the material (e.g. Dameron et al., 2015; Jarzabkowski & Kaplan, 2015; Werle & Seidl, 2015). Lê and Spee (2015) present four materiality approaches employed in organizational studies: communication; technology; sensemaking; positivism. The communication approach focuses on verbal, non-verbal and written text materials through which the organization is achieved, and on textual objects, physical locations of work and body – materiality relations. The technology approach incorporates the concept of *sociomateriality*, introduced by Orlikowski (2007), and directs attention to the relationships between technology, organization and people. The emerging sociomateriality theme in practice-based strategy research informs us that the social transpires through materials such as PowerPoint, cardboard cube, whiteboard and post-it notes, and through spatial arrangements, financial security and emotions (Balogun et al., 2014; Beech & Johnson, 2005; Cooren et al., 2015; Kaplan, 2011; Lê & Spee, 2015). Material agency is disclosed by strategy texts, affecting strategic planning through communicating meaning, guiding, disciplining and structuring discussions (Kaplan, 2011; Spee & Jarzabkowski, 2011; Vaara et al., 2010).

The sensemaking approach accounts for links between material and cognition, assuming that knowledge is embedded in materials that contain memory traces. Further, the approach examines how material interacts with interpretative processes and is used to drive behaviour. The positivist approach attends to materials defined by their physical qualities. It focuses on how materials influence and are influenced by human emotion, cognition and behaviour. Neuroscience methods are also employed by this approach to analyse underlying brain processes (Lê & Spee, 2015).

The materiality approaches raise our awareness of the importance of addressing the material in an organizational space. As Lê and Spee (2015, p. 582) highlight, 'spatial and material aspects are fundamental to accomplishing any organizational activity and process'. When elaborating on those aspects we must also make clear that material cannot be equated with materiality. The term 'material' derives from the Latin *mater* which means 'mother'; materials are 'the stuff that things are made of' and have nothing to do with materiality (Ingold, 2011, p. 20). Hodges (1976) provides us with rich information of material stuff such as wood, clay, stone, glass, leather, wool, copper, gold and silver and describes the processes that bring the flesh and blood of our bodies into corporeal contact with the material. For example, working with wood materials, felling trees, thinning out, cutting branches and if large enough using them as timber, involve the human body. By drawing on insights from Heidegger's (1962) hermeneutic-phenomenological work we are able to advance our understanding of the material and the spatial aspect in an existential meaning, accounting for a *being* of the timber material in its usability as expressed by a *readiness-to-hand* for house construction. From a Heideggerian view, materials are worked with and made use of in practice, attributed the character of tools (or equipment) which suggests describing socio-material practices as,

> open-ended human activities transpiring within material arrangements, unfolding in time and carried out by skilful agents whose actions are based on: tacit understandings, explicit rules and teleo-affective structures; the bodily coordination and orientation of an agent to the task at hand; and the incorporation of tools within the field of an agent's bodily comportment. (Tsoukas, 2015, pp. 62–3)

Heidegger's (1962) hermeneutic-phenomenological work helps us in problematizing the relationship between the material and the social through an approach that interweaves the social and the material with a concern for existential spatiality (Lamprou, 2017). As pointed out in this book, wood and other materials such as glass and stone, which each could be analysed for its physical properties, engage with business activities focused on maintenance and reconstruction, renewal and development of buildings and land. Materials are worked with, caught up in activities, in bodily doings used as tools for the performance and extension of activities in which family members and others find themselves.

Existential space is implied in the extension of activities. Materials are not, once and for all, fixed things that can be objectively identified by specific attributes, but bound up in business activities with which people entwine.

Activities also *take* place (Seamon, 2018). In appreciation of Heidegger's (1962) philosophy, geographical and anthropological studies have broadened the focus to include landscape in connection to 'place', addressing a bodily lived aspect of place (e.g. Casey, 2001; Ingold, 2011). Place describes a piece of land *scaped* by people, 'a textured composite' of materials grown and made (Ingold, 2011, p. 130). Under the name of Tällberg, place refers to a scaped land where present future-oriented business activities with which people are entwined recall past activities, reminding us of people not living any longer, their bodily doings and the paths made. Business activities are not performed within a geographical context and place-bound but place-binding through paths people have trailed and are trailing (Ingold, 2011).

Business activity is a dimension of practice and of a sociality that in Schatzki's (1996) terms denotes a vast *Zusammenhang* of lives, a hanging-togetherness (cf. Ericson, 2014), which involves genuinely related individuals.

INVOLVING GENUINELY RELATED INDIVIDUALS

Etymologically, 'social' stems from Latin *socialis*, which refers to companionship, allies, united and living together (*Etymology Dictionary*, 2020), examples of a hanging-togetherness to which can be added kinship. By definition, kinship is 'the network of genealogical relationships and social ties modelled on the relations of genealogical parenthood' (Holy, 1996, p. 40). Kinship directs us to 'family', a term that originally comes from Latin *familia* and the closely related term *famulus*, which means 'slave' (*Etymology Dictionary*, 2020). As Herlihy (1991, p. 3) informs: 'In classical Latin literature under the name of "family", there appear prostitutes in a brothel; publicans or tax collectors, moneyers; military units; schools of philosophers; and, in Christian usage, demons, monks, and the clergy generally.'

In medieval literature the notion of family conveyed an authoritarian structure as presented by a hierarchical order with a large group of people placed under the authority of a single person. Family was also presented as a domestic unity based on three sets of relationships, lord to servant,

husband to wife, and father to child. When the paternal authority weak-
ened, a domestic form emerged that allowed affection with love and
caritas (Latin for charity) to be expressed. Herlihy (1991, pp. 10–11)
summarizes: 'In this view, our love for these joined to us by blood relationships was founded on nature and was therefore stable and durable; in
contrast, our love for those unrelated to us was based on convention and
was unstable and shifting.'

More recent portrayals of family include a married heterosexual
couple and children, the so-called nuclear family, and in a wider sense,
a life process of collaborative engagement, emotional bonding and a joint
building of a shared reality, discourse, and institution (Hall, 2003).
'Family' denotes a form of living together that emerges through genuine
relationships based on blood and marriage. 'Genuine' also refers to
durable relationships established between friends and are characterized
by emotional bonding, 'reciprocity, mutual dependence and trust' (Hall,
2003, p. 33). The quality of genuine is not necessarily confined to interpersonal relationships between members of a family but includes also
particular well-known others such as friends, Sjöstrand (1997) explains.

Akin to genuine, and aligned with the extended family dimension,
affinal kin focuses on 'the emotional kinship groups, which could be
connected through descent or marriage and not purely genetics', Akhter
(2015, p. 179) points out. The stories presented in this book involve
individuals whose relationships are based on blood and marriage and cultivated on the basis of closeness and long-term interaction. It is important
to add that these genuinely related individuals are beings-in-the-world,
entwined with business activities in amongst materials spatially constituted and extended.

LISTENING TO STORIES

On the basis of a being-in-the-world narrative methodology, developed
from Ricoeur's (1992) conception of narrative and Heidegger's (1962)
conception of *Dasein* (Chapter 4), interpretation and understanding of
'family business' as activities are generated. A precise point of departure
based on a definition of family business that treats family and business
as distinct systems then is not of relevance to specify in advance. We
come to an understanding of the social and the material and their interwovenness when listening to people's stories about business activities.
Five stories evolve through the layering of voices belonging to family
members and others, dissolving family-owned hotels, a guest home

and a school, and owner and manager positions, into activities caught up in spatially related materials. The alternative approach – a theory of socio-material weaving – draws on people's stories about their activities and materials used as tools in an existential sense, and experienced in a bodily lived sense.

REMAINING CHAPTERS

Chapter 2 acknowledges that existing family business research directs considerable attention to the social dimension with reference to socio-emotional wealth, familiness, emotions, stewardship, cultural competence and entrepreneurship, for example. With succession in focus the social complexity of trans-generational change is explored. Without a concern for socio-material weaving scholars commonly refer to family business as a context attributed the characteristics of a system. The resource-based view and theories of social exchange, structural functionalism, symbolic interactionism, agency and evolution and a combination of theories explain what happens within the family business system and how it affects and is affected by the external environment. 'External environment' suggests the wider spatial context of industrial district, region and country in which scholars place the family business. Also noted, in business history research we are encountered with family businesses that operate and develop in continental, international and country-specific contexts.

Chapter 3 refers to the re-materializing of organizational life that is taking place in organization and management research, presenting three approaches: space as distance; space as materialization of power relations; space as lived experience. Integrated, these approaches account for scale of space in terms of micro, meso and macro levels. The chapter also points to a need for reflection on the ontological constitution of the social, and on the material in relation to spatiality, arguing that the philosophical tradition of hermeneutic phenomenology as represented by Heidegger (1962, 1971) provides concepts that could aid our understanding of spatiality. With reference to 'spatiality as care' it is acknowledged that material as *being*-things constitutes 'equipmentality', assigned theoretical and practical significance in human activity they contribute existential space. With reference to geographical and anthropological work informed by hermeneutic-phenomenological philosophy, 'place' is discussed in a bodily lived sense.

Chapter 4 focuses on narrative and story, placing a language-using storytelling human being, *homo narrans*, in the centre. Under the hermeneutic-phenomenological assumption of pre-narrative engagement in the world it suggests a being-in-the-world narrative methodology. As pointed out, intelligibility of being-in-the world expresses itself as discourse, language broken up in words constitutive of stories. The suggested methodology implies understanding and interpretation and allows for different temporal orientations and multiple plots to play out. The chapter also includes a description of how empirical-oriented information has been generated and how stories emerge through the involvement of individuals representing four families, emphasizing that the researcher is not an interviewer or observer, rather a 'story partner'. In between actualities and possibilities and with an account for what has been, stories emerge multivoicedly as voices of the living, the not living and the voice of the researcher blend.

Chapter 5 presents three stories in close relation to each other. The Siljanstrand and the Green Hotel story concentrate interest to first-generation activities and to the acquisition of a 'glittering jewel' and the realization of a 'San Michele dream'. The stories indicate that 'ownership' of Siljanstrand and Green Hotel unfolds owning activities with much attention focused on renewal and development of buildings and land. The Siljansgården story refers to a Tällberg land with grass fields, juniper and rose bushes and birch trees. It includes a three-generation family's involvement in activities oriented towards sports and recreation, education and guest home lodging. The activities open up to the social and the material, interwoven in the present with past activities recalled and a future imagined, highlighting a cultural achievement, a holistic treatment of body and soul, a 'co-worker for Life' and a beautiful Tällberg.

Chapter 6 presents the Klockargården story with reference to the five-generation Sandberg family. As exhibited, members representing the second, third and fourth generation have been intensely involved in business activities related to handicraft, sheep farming, textile education, guest home, hotel lodging, conferences and entertainment. The story tells that activities extend through materials associated with timbered buildings, many of which were bought, dismantled, moved from other places in Dalarna and rebuilt on the Klockargården land. Particular importance is ascribed the material of timber, which brings 'Nature' along, together with business activities constitutive of a nature-business wholeness. The chapter also refers to sorrows encumbered. It further acknowledges that

Klockargården has been sold and that the Sandberg family presently engages in the development of a project with business activities making land material available for presumptive buyers who wish to build a home in Tällberg and enjoy a beautiful view of Lake Siljan.

Chapter 7 presents the Åkerblads-Tällbergsgården story with reference to the 22-generation Åkerblad family. It illustrates Tällbergsgården hotel business activities in close relation to and as an extension of Åkerblads hotel business activities. Keeping alive the history of earlier generations of the Åkerblad family is a leitmotif applied throughout present future-oriented hotel business activities and is emphasized by the expression: 'the future is in history'. The story makes us aware that family members in their present entwinement with hotel business activities follow and connect with paths made by people not living any longer. A past unfolds in, between, through and around the old houses, cottages and *härbren*,[3] reminding us of earlier generations' engagement in farming activities. Owning and managing activities direct attention to maintenance and reconstruction, architectural and interior design that make use of materials such as timber, birch logs, glass, fine-grained metamorphic rock and candle wax.

Chapter 8 refers to the Siljanstrand, Siljansgården, Green Hotel, Klockargården and the Åkerblads-Tällbergsgården stories, directing attention to business activities caught up in materials that relate to spatiality as expressed by existential space and bodily lived place. From a hermeneutic-phenomenological perspective family business dissolves into activities with which people entwine in amongst materials. As pointed out, hermeneutic-phenomenological interpretation and understanding of the social and the spatial material shifts the focus away from entitized conceptions of family business contexts to 'entity' in the constitution of *entity-ness* accountable for *existence* and *being*. The chapter underlines the importance of adding to the study of family business, an alternative approach, in the form of a theory of socio-material weaving sensitive to a way of being in the world that implies an individual's entwinement with activity. In the discussion of the development of a socio-material weaving theory plausibility and a narrative truth are emphasized.

NOTES

1. Also in Tällbergs Byalag (2007, p. 8). My translation.
2. By definition, village is a group of houses usually located in the countryside (*Cambridge English Dictionary*, 2020).
3. A *härbre* is a small timbered storehouse.

2. Family business *as* contexts and *within* contexts

Existing research on family business is predominantly based on a systems view. As pointed out in this chapter, the family business system is conceived of as a context with considerable attention given to the social as reflected by conceptions such as emotional ownership, familiness and socioemotional wealth with little notion of the material in relation to space and place. Analyses framed by the resource-based view and theories of social exchange, structural functionalism, symbolic interactionism, agency, evolution and succession, and combinations of theories add to our understanding of the social. The spatiality of context is implied in systemic relationships between parts of the system and includes 'situational opportunities and constraints that affect the occurrence and meaning of organizational behavior as well as functional relationship between variables' (Johns, 2006, p. 386).

The chapter also acknowledges that the family business is surrounded by a wider context, the external environment. 'The verbal form – "to environ" – means to surround', informs Grange (1985, p. 78). As Nadel and Willner (1980, p. 218; emphasis in original) comment, context conveys *'the notion of something that surrounds and influences'*. Consistent with the systems view, under limited considerations of the spatial material, this wider context establishes a dual relationship with the family business. Family business scholars refer to industrial district, region and country (also in a multiple sense with reference to a cross-country context), in these different environments highlighting the sociality of human interactions and relations along with business-related factors. Business history scholars contribute empirical illustrations of family businesses that operate and develop 'across time and space' (Colli & Fernández Pérez, 2014, p. 277). The term 'space', which is often used interchangeably with the term 'place', is translated to continent, cross-country and country contexts, these contexts also seemingly ignorant of socio-material weaving.

AS CONTEXTS

Family business research opens up to a context that provides rich insights into the social. Characteristics of the family business context are primarily set in social terms with little notion of the material. Family business is an organizational context that shapes and is shaped by workplace relationships that tie family and non-family actors to one another (Waldkirch, 2018). 'As an integrated system, the family business is a business context characterized by genuine relations', adds Hall (2003, p. 50). It is a context that inspires researchers to elaborate on culture, factors that affect culture, and effects caused by cultural processes (Fletcher et al., 2012), meaning and power (Adiguna, 2015) and gender relations (Staffansson Pauli, 2015), for example. Spanning individual, family and organizational levels, the conceptions of emotional ownership, familiness and socioemotional wealth determine the uniqueness of the family business system in its alleged entirety.

Emotional ownership refers to cognitive and affective states that account for a family member's attachment to and identification with the family business (Björnberg & Nicholson, 2012). Familiness is a particular form of social capital (Pearson et al., 2008) and is closely related to family firm identity (Zellweger et al., 2010) and emotions (Brundin & Sharma, 2012). It involves 'the idiosyncratic firm level bundle of resources and capabilities resulting from the systems interactions' (Habbershon et al., 2003, p. 451). According to Brundin and Sharma (2012), familiness is produced by emotional messiness, which implies contradictory emotions that contingent on the family's emotional intelligence generate both positive and negative outcomes. Familiness builds on hybrid identities, psychological ownership (underlying which are self-efficacy, self-identity and a feeling of belongingness) and psychological contracts that include promises and expectations. Since family businesses consist of 'two different organizations in one – the family and the business', they are characterized as hybrid identities (Brundin & Sharma, 2012, p. 55), implicating family as a normative system of values and altruism, and business as a utilitarian system founded in profit maximization and self-interest.

Socioemotional wealth 'known as "affective endowments" – is generally referred to as the noneconomical utilities derived by principals (i.e., the family) from a business', submit Brigham and Payne (2019, p. 326). In behavioural terms studies explain how family firms behave to avoid the loss of socioemotional wealth (e.g. Gomez-Mejia et al., 2007), in dispositional terms studies measure the importance of socioemotional wealth to family members, mirrored by their preferences for certain strategic behaviour of the firm (e.g. Debicki et al., 2016). Lacking a precise definition, studies include multiple dimensions of socioemotional wealth and point also to its 'bright' and 'dark' sides. Berrone et al. (2012, p. 259) refer to 'the unrestricted exercise of personal authority vested in family members, the enjoyment of family influence over the business, and close identification with the firm that usually carries the family's name'. With a focus on the relationship between socioemotional wealth and financial performance, Naldi et al. (2013) highlight a bright and a dark side, underlining the importance of achieving a fit between socioemotional objectives and the environment, defined by institutional attributes of informal and formal rules. Socioemotional wealth is described in a positive way as an asset family CEOs can use when informal rules prevail and in a negative way as a liability when the environment is characterized by formal rules. Researchers further show that different dimensions of socioemotional wealth such as family control and influence, identification with the firm, social ties, emotional attachment and succession correspond to resources that help in dealing with stressors. Stressors result from mental disorders that might arise and affect family and work systems that overlap in family businesses, as Miller et al. (2020) inform. Socioemotional wealth originates in and develops through socialization processes that include 'exposure to and interactions with both family and business systems from a very young age', summarize Murphy et al. (2019, p. 412).

Richness in Theoretical Approaches

Family business as context implicates an integrated system whose features are essentially social in character as illustrated above. Few studies adopt a theoretical approach that deviates from an approach spawned by systems theory. Strongly critical of the systems view, Helin (2011) presents family business as a context for dialogues between family members with the emphasis on performativity. Bridging process organization studies with Bakhtin's (e.g. 1981) work on dialogue, she attends to a family business context in which family members do their family and business work in language.

Edited by prominent family business scholars, handbooks supply comprehensive overviews of the literature on family business, informing about a rich variety of theoretical approaches which, for the most part, introduce family business as a system (e.g. De Massis et al., 2012; Melin et al., 2014; Nordqvist et al., 2015; Smyrnios et al., 2014; Sorenson et al., 2015; Zellweger, 2017). 'The unique feature of the family business field is that scholars focus on investigating and understanding the reasons, meaning, role and impact of the interaction between at least two systems; the family and the business', assert Nordqvist et al. (2015, p. 1). Theory that links the social to the material with a concern for space and place does not receive much interest. As exemplified in the following, the resource-based view and theories of social exchange, structural function-alism, symbolic interactionism and agency are adopted with attention mainly directed to the social. Studies applying evolutionary theory and those concentrating on succession tend also to leave out a material spatial dimension as exhibited henceforth. Despite richness in theoretical approaches there is little recognition of family business as socio-material weaving.

The resource-based view 'sweeping through the field of family busi-nesses' (Rau, 2014, p. 321) explains how a family firm's unique bundle of resources is tied to competitive advantage (Habbershon et al., 2003). From this view, the family business system is characterized by the idio-syncratic resource of familiness (Habbershon & Williams, 1999), which builds on structural, cognitive and relationship dimensions of social capital (Pearson et al., 2008), also referred to as family social capital (cf. Chirico & Salvato, 2016). Family social capital is a unique asset defined by 'the sum of all actual and potential resources stemming from rela-tionships between family members within family firms' (Herrero, 2018, p. 441). Positively associated with a market-oriented culture (Tokarcyk et al., 2007), the resource of familiness is leveraged through marketing, influencing the firm's wealth creation, performance and generation of competitive advantage (Blombäck & Craig, 2014). By combining the resource-based view with the knowledge-based view, Carbrea-Suárez et al. (2001) broaden the perspective to include capabilities developed through complex interactions among the firm's resources with routines used for integrating, coordinating and mobilizing resources and capabili-ties (cf. Kammerlander & Holt, 2018).

Social exchange theory incorporates a market concept, maintaining that individuals motivated by self-interest make decisions that help max-imize their gains and limit their losses (Jennings et al., 2014). Moreover, it accounts for mechanisms and outcomes of family members' interac-tions (Cropanzano & Mitchell, 2005). In short, social exchange theory explains how economic and social factors govern, enable and constrain the allocation of resources and how the exchange of valuable tangible and intangible resources occurs within the social system of family business (Daspit et al., 2016).

Structural functionalism, originating in the need to assure the citizens of stability and safety within the post-war society (Parsons, 1951 [1970]), opens the family business system to a conception of families as biological, social or legal entities. Interlinked with stewardship theory (Le Breton-Miller & Miller, 2009), structural functionalism focuses on individuals' spousal roles and career choices and on child socialization. Stewardship theory originates in the idea that the manager has a strong sense of duty towards the organization, its well-being and performance (Davis et al., 1997; Miller & Le Breton-Miller, 2006). It is most commonly associated with emotional attachment and benevolent behaviour. Yet, it is 'not particularly prone to explain and capture benevolent behaviour in organizations due to its utilitarian core and disregard for interpersonal benevolence', inject Waldkirch and Nordqvist (2017, p. 407).

Symbolic interactionism (Blumer, 1969; Mead, 1932) is about how individuals' meanings arise in social interactions, vary depending on roles, values and norms, and how meanings are communicated in the family and the firm (Carr & Sequira, 2007; Nordqvist, 2005). Combining symbolic interactionism with cultural theory, Hall and Nordqvist (2008) open up the family business context to an extended notion of professional management. By moving beyond the traditional meaning of formal qualifications achieved through education and training, they show that cultural competence, concerning both the general family business level and the level of the daily management practice, is integral to professional management. Cultural competence 'means an understanding of the owner family's goals and meanings of being in business, that is, the values and norms underlying the reason for it being in business' (Hall & Nordqvist, 2008, p. 59).

Agency theory, dominating the study of family governance (Goel et al., 2014), directs attention to 'a set of agency relations within and between the family system, ownership system and the business system' (Van den Berghe & Carchon, 2003, p. 171). It elicits that family firms have lower owner-manager costs than non-family firms (Chrisman et al., 2004). A desired outcome of agency theory is cost minimization and greater efficiency (Madison et al., 2017a). 'A notable feature of family firms is they are often founded as "high trust" organizations that benefit greatly from reduced agency costs', remark Steier and Muethel (2014,

p. 499). Agency problems still arise, especially in a family business where ownership is dispersed among the members of the family (Schulze et al., 2003). Conjoined with social exchange theory, agency theory recognizes agency of intermediate status, which includes family members not holding a position as owner or manager, so-called latent principals. Intertwined with stewardship theory, agency theory is used for examining how agency and stewardship governance affects the behaviour on the individual level and the performance on the firm level (cf. Le-Breton Miller & Miller, 2018; Madison et al., 2017a). Behavioural agency theory (Mazzelli, 2015) based on socioemotional wealth of the family aims to understand the risk behaviour of family firms (Kumeto, 2015).

Evolutionary theory integrates resource-based theory with agency and stewardship theories, supplying 'explanatory content to the concept of interest in agency theory, to the notion of family capital in resource-based theory, and to the source of values that are central to stewardship theory', explains Nicholson (2014, p. 132). Framed by evolutionary theory, studies of the family business system direct attention to interactions between the organization and the environment with respect to variation, selection and retention processes through which resources are secured (Nicholson, 2014). The theory draws on the neo-Darwinian concepts of 'modification by descent' and 'reproductive fitness' implied in which is the belief that certain 'design' features are eliminated or retained over generations and that genes are replicated through natural selection (Nicholson, 2008, p. 108). Because of humans' evolutionary origins, the family as 'a key social entity in biology' is close to work, forming an economic unit that based on kinship promotes trans-generational responsibility (Nicholson, 2014, p. 119).

Applying evolutionary theory in psychology, integrated with research on socioemotional wealth, Yu et al. (2020) too regard family as a fundamental biological unit and a building block of society. They hold that motivation to preserve socioemotional wealth varies depending on close and distant kinship. 'Close kin are parents, siblings, and one's children. Distant kin are other family relations including grandparents, aunts/uncles, nephews/nieces, cousins, and in-laws' (Yu et al., 2020, p. 135). Close genetic ties afford stronger emotional attachment and provision of support and loyalty, which transferred to the family firm help maintain socioemotional wealth. The succession process might also require non-kin support. The adaptive capacity required for spurring long-term growth and assuring survival of a family unit builds on teamwork and coalitions between kin and non-kin (Nicholson, 2008).

Evolutionary theory points us in the direction of succession, which is one of the most studied topics of family business and a particularly critical one as many family businesses do not survive beyond the first generation (e.g. Daspit et al., 2016; Evert et al., 2016; Haag, 2012). With succession in focus, studies examine a family business context of life cycles, and complex processes of human interaction that do not coincide with the linearity of a life cycle. Succession studies of what goes on within the family business context contribute insights into the social in relation to knowledge, entrepreneurial orientation, emotions and the human relational as acknowledged in the following.

With Succession in Focus

One typology describing family business succession is the life cycle (e.g. Gersick et al., 1997; Peiser & Wooten, 1983). Life cycles studies used to include biology-inspired applications based on stage models for the intro-duction, growth, maturity and decline of a single product or organization (Hoy, 2014). 'Humanizing the process, rather than a simple litany of facts and dates, brings the history to life for those who follow', emphasizes Hoy (2014, p. 624), arguing that the history should include the external and internal factors that lead to a firm's survival and success. On the basis of the life cycle, history contains periods of change and stability that the family business system goes through when involved in succession.

Family business succession implies trans-generational (intrafamily or intergenerational) change, a complex process in which management and ownership issues are tightly intertwined (Haag et al., 2006). 'The succession process is often construed to encompass the actions, events, and organizational mechanisms by which leadership at the top of the firm, and often ownership are transferred', clarify Le Breton-Miller et al. (2014, p. 305). Succession takes the family business from an initiation stage, through integration and joint management of the predecessor and the successor, to a final stage where leadership is assumed by the suc-cessor (e.g. Cadieux et al., 2002; Ibrahim et al., 2001). The whole family business system, 'inherently complex due to the interdependency of family, ownership, and business life cycles as well as to these operating and evolving simultaneously within the subsystems of the whole entity', moves from one developmental stage to another, explains Murray (2003, p. 18). With the stages corresponding to the archetypical family business structures, defined by controlling ownership, sibling partnership and cousin consortium, ownership becomes successively dispersed (Murray, 2003).

The succession process is generally initiated and controlled by the incumbent (a family member holding the top management position), whose desire is to keep the business in the family. The incumbent's attitude towards intrafamily succession is a most critical individual-level determinant of succession, according to De Massis et al. (2016). It is affected by situational and individual antecedents as regards, for instance, number of children and family shareholders, perceived positive firm performance and emotional attachment. At an early stage of succession, stewardship attitude as expressed through altruism and conjoined with agency rationales can help regulate conflict of interest and enable the creation of a shared vision of future ownership, add Meier and Schier (2016). The difference between generalized and restricted exchange between the incumbent and the successor is also important to consider as Daspit et al. (2016) point out from a social exchange perspective. The former type of exchange refers to indirect reciprocity and long-term obligations based on trust, loyalty and respect, and the latter is more instrumental, entailing direct reciprocity and expectations of short-term returns.

A more recent contribution to the discussion on the incumbent–successor relationships is the 'theory of succession in family firms'. On the basis of a microeconomic (mathematical) analysis Giménez and Novo (2020) present a theory that considers all available choices an incumbent can take in a succession process. The theory accounts for the role of effectiveness of education, training and experience of the successor, and the role of personal traits and non-monetary incentives of the incumbent and the potential successor. Key elements include the incumbent's reluctance to step aside, underperforming succession, barriers to non-family succession and the role of trust embedded in the honesty dimension of the succession process.

Trans-generational change also involves knowledge processes and networks, attempts to maintain and strengthen entrepreneurial orientation, and emotions expressed through compassion, dissonance, historicization processes and familial solidarity as indicated next.

Knowledge, entrepreneurial orientation and emotions
The exchange between the predecessor and the successor is subjected to analyses that focus on knowledge transfer, evolutionary and internalizing knowledge processes. Knowledge transfer is enabled by the predeces-

sor's motivation to delegate and grant the successor managerial discretion (Kammerlander & Holt, 2018) and entails, in addition, a transfer of idiosyncratic knowledge developed within the community where the family firm is located and interacts with other family firms (Bjuggren & Sund, 2001). The transfer of knowledge in conjunction with the transition of roles (Daspit et al., 2016) is 'a mutual role adjustment process', Handler (1994, p. 136) notes, meaning that it might take the predecessor longer to move into his changed role, from sole operator to a consultant, who disengages or retires from the business. Extending the knowledge-transfer perspective, Carbrea-Suárez et al. (2018) describe knowledge exchange as an evolutionary process that includes a knowledge network of contacts with non-family employees and different stakeholders. Chirico and Salvato (2016) highlight internalization of knowledge. They purport that family social capital, affective commitment and relationship conflicts influence a family firm's ability to internalize its members' knowledge, which refers to the ability of family members to recognize, assimilate and exploit each other's knowledge.

In addition to knowledge transfer between generations, and evolutionary and internalizing knowledge processes, entrepreneurial orientation is a theme that has gained attention in studies of succession. Astrachan et al. (2008) present 'most quote papers' on family business research, revealing that family business entrepreneurship has emerged as one of the most dynamic research themes. From an entrepreneurial perspective succession entails entrepreneurial entry of new owners and entrepreneurial exit of old owners (Nordqvist et al., 2013). This suggests processes through which familiness, the family's entrepreneurial mindset and capabilities are transferred across generations and contribute to renewal (Basco et al., 2019; Cruz & Nordqvist, 2012). At the mature stage of the firm's life cycle, the founder-entrepreneur most likely loses entrepreneurial capacity as Hall et al. (2001) point out. To be entrepreneurial, engaging in continuous improvement while keeping up with the speed of change in the firm's environment, the firm must have an explicit and open culture that actively encourages actions to break away from the old (Hall et al., 2001). Family firms behave entrepreneurially by engaging in innovative behaviour, mobilizing idiosyncratic features. They leverage on the family culture and 'use the stock of business acumen accumulated over generations to decipher customer needs to innovate', Dibrell et al. (2017, p. 276) maintain. Erdogan et al. (2020) submit that temporal symbiosis is a capability a family firm must be endowed with to be able to encourage change while simultaneously promoting continuity through preserving tradition across generations. Entrepreneurial trans-generational transfer of practices actualizes also moral emotions of compassion (Akhter et al., 2016). These emotions matter when transforming socioemotional wealth and practices from one generation to another, motivating continued growth and entrepreneurship, concludes Akhter (2016).

Emotions play a major role in trans-generational change (e.g. Björnberg & Nicholson, 2012; Brundin & Sharma, 2012). At each succession stage, emotional dissonance could emerge due to differences in the ways in which individuals express and actually experience emotions (Labaki et al., 2013). Bridging business history research, Holt and Popp (2013, p. 905) view family as a constellation of emotions, 'a site of powerful emotional experiences, processes and settlements'. They propose a historicization of emotions which encompasses inward and outward enaction of emotions in a succession process. Inward enaction implies a micro perspective that includes an individual's experiences and interpretations, self-awareness and awareness of others, and outward enaction a macro perspective that refers to the wider social and institutional context that influences the family firm's reputation, commercial success, traditions and ethics. Also the life course perspective proposed by Bengtson and Allen (1993, p. 470) provides micro-macro linkages as the family is understood as 'a micro-social group within a macro-social context, a collection of individuals within a shared history who interact within ever-changing social contexts across ever-changing time and space'.

Contextually, the life course perspective addresses heterogeneity in structure and processes, acknowledging the individual's and the family's location in a changing societal environment. Szydlik (2012, p. 100) clarifies: 'On the one hand, societal contexts influence lifelong intergenerational behavior. On the other hand, family solidarity may have strong consequences for societies at large.' Familial solidarity refers to emotional and functional bonds between generations. Murphy et al. (2019) add that socioemotional wealth, conceptualized as an individual frame of mind formed by a sense of belonging to and identification with the family business, affects the life courses of the next-generation family members and the continuity of the family business.

Emphasizing the human relational
Applying a strategizing perspective, Haag et al. (2006) elevate the micro aspect of succession while accounting for communicative practices and power expressed through human relations and interactions. From a communicative perspective the future comes into view when the members of

the family decide on a course of action (cf. Helin, 2011). In this family business context the 'present moment' is essential; it is a living moment where 'everything is happening, where utterances emerge in an unpredictable yet, dialogically shaped way, enabling transformation to occur', posit Helin and Jabri (2015, p. 501).

Philosophically inspired by the sociology of practice and based on a strategy-as-practice perspective, Haag (2012, p. 65) probes further into the relational succession process, purporting it could include an element of 'detectable purposiveness' without being deliberately planned and measured in relation to the financial performance of the business. She examines the ongoing internal socialization process through which family members continuously exchange experiences and learn. Parental values, beliefs and experiences that shape the socialization of the child serve as an intergenerational influence agent, according to Carr and Sequira (2007). Socialization in later generations is dependent on the successor's interactions with stakeholders and peers and on changes occurring over time in the family and in the firm (Bika et al., 2019). On the basis of the analysis of succession as an internal socialization process, Haag (2012, p. 189) considers two aspects to be focal for the family business, 'first, a family harmony that allows family members to work creatively together while appreciating individuality; second, managing the duality of preservation and renewal so that the essence of the business is preserved, yet expressed in new ways'. Preservation in its past orientation is considered simultaneously with renewal in its future orientation.

Organizational characteristics provide context for the family, and the external environment for the organization, assert Cappelli and Scherer (1991). In the following, examples are provided of external environments as 'within contexts'.

WITHIN CONTEXTS

Industrial district, region and country describe a spatiality that refers to external environments, that is, contexts within which family businesses are located and operate. With a focus on the business environment of industrial districts in Italy, Naldi et al. (2013) examine the relationship between socioemotional wealth and financial performance in family-controlled firms (as mentioned earlier). Industrial districts are defined as 'clusters of geographically proximate firms in the same or closely related industries, characterized by a unique interfirm collaboration; webs of relationships; and social, unwritten norms' (Naldi et al.,

2013, p. 1345). In the industrial district of Gnosjö in Sweden, Wigren (2003) identifies four arenas: the business firm; the business-related activities; the church; the local theatre association. Arena is described as a sphere of interest and activity. From a social constructionist perspective with the emphasis placed on the socio-cognitive dimension of culture, she explores networks of meanings that emotively manifest in values and norms, revealing that there are 'value pairs' allowing inclusion and exclusion, cooperation and competition, equality and inequality among people interacting on an arena.

Region is presented as a spatial context demarcated by regional factors and processes that comprise local economic and social actors (Basco, 2015). The recent cross-fertilization between region development research and family business research (Stough et al., 2015) has brought regional family firm embeddedness and familiness to the fore with an explicit concern for region as a spatial context. Regional factors refer to physical, human and social capital, and regional processes to information exchange, learning, social interaction, competitive and institutional change and to spatial proximity defined by geographical, cognitive, social, organizational and institutional dimensions (Basco, 2015).

Showing an interest in the Gulf region (encompassing the countries of Bahrain, Kuwait, Qatar, Oman, Saudi Arabia and the United Arab Emirates), Davis et al. (2000) inform about a business environment where family companies, characterized by long-term visions, relationships and investments and by a strong concern for their communities, are faced with changes pertaining to distribution technology, decreased government support, privatization and demographics. A new generation of business and community leaders allow for greater workplace diversity, collaborative and decentralized organizations. The Gulf region can be viewed 'as a grand space or spatial crossroads in exchange, trade, diffusion and connectivity between a set of grand source areas to the south, north and east', contends Agnew (2011, p. 317). The Anglic, Germanic and Nordic regions are in the centre of the study of Gupta et al. (2011) of family business characteristics and differences as regards a family's involvement in the business. McMillan Lequieu (2015, p. 45) focuses on German-heritage farmers in Wisconsin, a region in the United States of 'rich agricultural soil, protected wetland, and proximity to urban sprawl'.

It needs to be added that a stream of entrepreneurship research (e.g. Müller & Korsgaard, 2017; Welter, 2011) have contributed insights into various aspects of context. With a focus on emerging economies and developing countries, Ramirez Pasillas et al. (2017) examine entrepreneurship as a contextualized phenomenon. In agreement with Welter (2011) they hold that economic behaviour can be understood within the context of social, spatial, institutional or societal norms. In a study of women's entrepreneurship Welter et al. (2014, p. 2) explain how the spatial relates to the social:

> Social context includes the relations of individuals, be their networks, families, households or friends. The spatial context covers the physical and geographical environment, the institutional context the regulatory and normative environment. These contexts overlap; for example the social context (the networks, family, and households) and the institutional context (laws, norms, regulations) both have a spatial dimension.

Context provides opportunities and barriers for entrepreneurial behaviour (Welter, 2011). With reference to a rural setting in Denmark, Müller and Korsgaard (2017) show how different levels of spatial embeddedness influence different types of entrepreneurial activities. It is particularly interesting to note that they incorporate a material aspect, conceptualizing spatial context as a socio-material phenomenon. Spatial context is 'the location of entrepreneurial ventures with its socio-material aspects delimited by natural or geographical boundaries such as e.g. mountains, valleys or waters as well as socio-cognitive boundaries such as communities or neighbourhoods and locationally bounded representations and meanings' (Müller & Korsgaard, 2017, p. 227). As pointed out, material is both enabling and constraining entrepreneurial activities.

Addressing Country and Cross-Country

Baù et al. (2013) conducted a comprehensive review of scholarly family business literature, published since the mid-1970s on the topic of ownership and management succession and identified also cross-country studies. They argue that the country context, constituted of economic, firm demographics and cultural-institutional factors, is important for the evolution of ownership succession. Fletcher et al. (2012) also refer to the country context, evaluations of which elicit that national-level cultural attitudes affect family business behaviour. Within the country context of Germany, ownership, corporate governance and management of family businesses and non-family businesses are examined (Klein, 2000; cf. Pieper et al., 2008). Moreover, studies analyse value differences among family firms in Spain (Simon et al., 2012), the relationship between socioemotional wealth and financial performance in family-controlled firms in Italy (Naldi et al., 2013), how long-established family firms in the craft industry in Turkey manage the tension between tradition and innovation (Erdogan et al., 2020), socialization processes occurring across generations in Scottish family firms (Bika et al., 2019), the ability and willingness of Canadian family firms to engage in R&D investments (Bozec & Di Vito, 2019) and entrepreneurial cultures in family businesses in Honduras (Discua Cruz et al., 2012). Other examples of 'within-country' research include analyses of financial performance and financial structures of family businesses and non-family businesses in Japan (Allouche et al., 2008), the impact of family businesses on the economy of the United States (Astrachan & Shanker, 2003) and on the economic development of China and share in social responsibilities (Xi et al., 2016).

An important contribution to our understanding of contexts is Akhter's (2016) study of portfolio entrepreneurship in the country context of Pakistan. It makes the dimension of spatiality explicit in connection to the social context of portfolio entrepreneurship. Akhter (2016, p. 23) defines portfolio entrepreneurship as 'family owning multiple businesses involved in multiple related or unrelated diversified business activities in addition to their core legacy business'. He examines the processes through which the business portfolio grows and contracts, how the portfolio endures, what entrepreneurial strategies it engages and what processes underlie exit strategies in cases where business families in the face of decline strive to preserve their portfolio across generations. The study includes both rural and urban spatial and social contexts. In rural-based firms, business families tend to encourage organic growth whereas in urban-based firms they are more inclined to grow the portfolio through acquisitions and joint ventures. Akhter (2016) stresses the importance of trans-generational moral emotions in transferring socioemotional wealth and practices from one generation to another, sustaining the legacy of the business family.

Moreover, researchers provide information about the characteristics of and differences between family businesses in a cross-country context. Studies include comparisons of strategic behaviour, managers' values and attitudes, environment, objects, internal characteristics and performance of family businesses and non-family businesses in Austria, Belgium, Germany, Finland, France, the United Kingdom, the Netherlands and Switzerland (Donckels & Fröhlich, 1991). Further, studies pay attention to entrepreneurial family businesses in Latin America (e.g. Botero & Betancourt, 2016; Nordqvist et al., 2011), and in the Asia Pacific (Au et al., 2011), compare family and non-family firms that operate in the United States, Germany, Switzerland, China, Brazil and India (Jennings et al., 2015), assess the social and economic impact of the family business in the United Kingdom, Germany and Spain (Welch, 1991), explain differences between Chinese and Japanese business firms with reference to socio-cultural-political traditions and institutions (Chau, 1991) and family business planning for succession in a seven-country study encompassing Croatia, Egypt, France, India, Kosovo, Kuwait and the United States (Lussier & Sonfield, 2012).

Since 'family business' has been included as a prominent subfield of business history (Colli, 2003) it is noteworthy to get a glimpse of what business historians have done. Space, often used interchangeably with place, refers to continental, international and country-specific contexts family businesses are surrounded by and interact with. According to Colli and Fernández Pérez (2014, p. 277) a business history approach 'provides an articulated kaleidoscope of cases which are useful in order to interpret many of the features which the present family firms show across the globe, and contribute to a better conceptualisation of what family businesses are in reality, across space and time'.

A Business History Perspective

Alfred D. Chandler Jr (1918–2007) is a recognized scholar in business history. In research on the growth and development of large manufacturing firms in the United States, he elevated the role of organization and professional management in the performance of firms (Jones & Zeitlin, 2008). In reaction to Chandler's (e.g. 1962, 1977) emphasis on the superiority of professionally managed firms, business historians more recently have brought growth and development of family businesses to the fore, exhibiting that firms owned and managed by families are found in modern scale-intensive industries (Colli, 2003). Through a study of the performance of Dutch family firms, covering the period 1890 to 1940, Sluyterman and Winkelman (1993) demonstrate that family firms and personal relationships play a crucial role in industrial development. Dutch industrial capitalism is described as personal capitalism and as family capitalism, clearly distinguished from Chandler's managerial capitalism. Jones and Rose's (1993) collection of essays on family firms operating in the United States, Europe and Asia also inform about family firms as being efficient and capable of adapting to a changing environment.

With the focus on multigenerational family dynasties, referred to as 'multigenerational families with several branches and successful business portfolios' (Jaffe & Laine, 2004, p. 81) and family capitalism (James, 2006), scholars compare family businesses operating in the continents of the United States, Europe and Asia. Surveying and assessing existing historiography and analyses of family businesses in these continents since the 1960s, Colli and Rose (2008, p. 195) point to 'the shifting nature in family capitalism and the changes in the economic contribution and management of family firms through time and space'. In Europe, James (2006) follows the historical trajectories in the eighteenth and nineteenth centuries of three families, the Wendels in France, the Haniels in Germany and the Falcks in Italy. His comparison gives detailed information on how the Wendels engaged in the iron and steel industry, the Haniels in the metallurgical and trading businesses and the Falcks in the steel industry, and on their active contribution to European industrialization.

The presence of the family firm in business history studies is also closely tied to economic and social strengths identified in the context of a specific country. Sweden, Switzerland, Germany, India and China are examples of such a context as illustrated below.

In the country of Sweden, Sjögren (2018) directs attention to the evolution of family dynasties such as Bonniers, Wallenberg, Kamprad and Rausing. Lindgren (2002) focuses specifically on the Wallenberg dynasty in terms of a sphere of companies with viability through five generations. Directing attention to Switzerland, Dejung (2013) demonstrates that the family business Volkart Bros, founded in 1851, became one of the biggest merchant houses in South Asia. For as long as a century it maintained a leading position in the export of Indian raw cotton to Europe. Also interested in the country-specific environment of Switzerland, Ginalski (2013, p. 985) concentrates on large firms in the Swiss machine, electro-technical and metallurgy sectors, making a distinction between family-owned and family-controlled firms with family control defined as 'strong family capitalism'.

Germany and capitalism are at the centre of Berghoff's (2006) study of changes that took place in the *Mittelstand* sector after World War II from 1949 through 2000. This sector consists of small and medium-sized family-owned firms characterized by 'strong emotional investment by owners and staff, and an emphasis on continuity, paternalism, and independence' (Berghoff, 2006, p. 264). In a study of Bertelsmann in Germany, Europe's largest media company, covering the period

1950–2010, Berghoff (2013, p. 855) concentrates on 'the structure of the family, the remodelling of ownership and controlling right, the methods of finance, and the role of non-family managers'. He presents empirical evidence for a hybrid form of governance as the line between family and non-family manager successively blurred, blending family and managerial capitalism.

In the country of India, Chittoor and Das (2007) investigate large family business groups, their succession processes and professionalization of management. In a study of eighteenth-century commercial family firms in the Indian city of Bombay, Smith (1993) specifically attends to family firm networks as products of Hindu values associated with collectively felt responsibility for continuity within the family and the firm. Susanto and Susanto (2013) focus on Chinese family businesses and the roles they play in the mainland and overseas in the countries of Indonesia, Thailand, Malaysia, Singapore and the Philippines. The way Chinese business is done is strongly influenced by 'familism' interlinked with Confusian values, filial piety and *quanxi*. Confusian values accentuate qualities of commitment, collective responsibility and an individual's concern for the welfare of others. Filial piety implies respect for older people, and *quanxi* entails long-term connections between people and networks of contacts (Susanto & Susanto, 2013).

IN SUMMATION

As acknowledged in this chapter there is limited concern for a material spatial dimension in family business research. Spatiality is rather equated with 'context' in the narrow sense of 'family business' and in the wider sense of 'external environment'. Family business is commonly approached as a system which in terms of context allows the social to be expressed through family ties, genuine relations, culture, meaning, power, gender and emotions. Theoretical frameworks help us to understand aspects of the social that relate to idiosyncrasies of resources and capabilities, allocation and exchange of resources, stewardship, individuals' spousal roles, career choices, child socialization, cultural competence, agency and governance and to an adaptive capacity of the family unit. With family described as a key social entity in biology, the social borders on neo-Darwinism.

With reference to succession as sequential stages of a life cycle and as relational and socializing processes, social dynamics are highlighted through a focus on the incumbent and the successor, knowledge, entrepreneurial orientation, emotions, communicative practices, living moments, exchanges of experiences and learning. As indicated, succession occurs within the predefined context of the family business system with the subsystems of family, business and ownership (or family, ownership and management) affording complex structural and relational intersections and overlaps that elevate the social without much consideration for how the social relates to the material.

As the chapter further acknowledges, family business scholars address industrial district, region, country and cross-country contexts, and business history scholars address continental, international and country-specific contexts. The exemplified contexts define external environments in which a variety of factors that supposedly lie outside of the family business are joined together, shaping and being shaped by the family business. This actualizes the etymological meaning of the word 'context', which derived from Latin *contextus* means 'a joining together' (*Etymology Dictionary*, 2020). The external environmental within contexts seem to be effective in enabling and constraining factors such as economic, demographic, cultural and institutional for family business operations. Environmental-level studies investigate 'the impact of factors external to the firm, such as financial and legal institutional and national cultures', summarize Baù et al. (2013, p. 172).

Family business *as* contexts and *within* contexts appears to leave little room for the spatial in its material constitution and extension. It is important to note, though, that Akhter (2016) in the study of portfolio entrepreneurship in rural- and urban-based family firms in Pakistan, and Basco (2015) with a focus on regional factors and processes, make a spatial context explicit in conjunction with a social context. Basco (2015), moreover, includes the aspect of spatial proximity, defined by geographical, cognitive, social, organizational and institutional dimensions. As also pointed out, a stream of entrepreneurship research makes the spatial explicit and explores spatial context as a socio-material phenomenon. Spatial proximity communicates information on spatial distance (cf. Taylor & Spicer, 2007). Wigren's (2003) analysis of value pairs actualizes the proximity and distance aspects of spatiality as reflected by differences in arena actors' socio-cognitive expressions and relations.

'Context' requires more attention, purport Baù et al. (2013). There is, in addition, a need for moving beyond the 'within' character of context and make context less abstract through 'materializing' context with reference to space and place. Context is often endowed with an objectness that tends to hinder an understanding of how materials involve *with* activity and enable spatial extension (cf. Ingold, 2011). Context is not only 'there' to situate, embed or surround an agent such as a family business, and family business is not a predefined systems context awaiting an analysis of the social but activities that bring the social and the material together and extend beyond the boundaries of a system and a context, the internal and the external. As Zeitlin (2008, p. 125) argue we should not accept a rigid distinction between agent and context and we should deny giving 'any ontological and epistemological privilege to the individual business firm as the key unit of analysis and economic governance.'

For the development of an alternative approach that brings socio-material weaving to the fore it is necessary to leave 'context' more open for the social in conjunction with the material to extend as people involve in business activities. As emphasized in the ensuing chapter, we should also break up the totemic relationship between space and place, in consideration of the existential and the bodily lived appreciate the difference between space and place.

3. Social and material, space and place

From the entry into a discussion of organizational space with the social and the material conceived of as related spheres of organizational life, the chapter moves on to include a notion of spatiality that allows for differentiation between space and place, offering an existential interpretation of space and a bodily lived interpretation of place. The lack of socio-material perspectives in family business research prompts us to look elsewhere to gain insights into the social as it interweaves with the material. Most germane to a study of family business are socio-material approaches employed by studies that align around organization and management practices. The chapter notes that a re-materializing of organizational life is taking place in organization and management research and presents three approaches: space as distance; space as materialization of power relations; space as lived experience. Integrated these approaches account for scale of space in terms of micro, meso and macro levels.

As the chapter also points out, the philosophical tradition of hermeneutic phenomenology as represented by Heidegger (1962, 1971) suggests a way to think about spatiality, the social and the material. The chapter pays particular regard to 'spatiality as care', bringing existential space to the fore with the Heideggerian notion of *Dasein* designating a human's being-in-the-world, emphasizing a human's entwinement with activities in amongst materials. Moreover, the chapter acknowledges that some studies of geography and anthropology draw on insights from Heidegger's (1962) work. The attentional focus broadens to include landscape in connection to 'place'. As opposed to space, place opens up to experiential exploration of a world of materials that makes salient the bodily lived.

RELATED SPHERES OF ORGANIZATIONAL LIFE

Social and material aspects of organizational space have increasingly received interest from organization and management theorists (e.g. Binder & Hellström, 2005; Dale & Burrell, 2008; Hernes, 2004; Kornberger & Clegg, 2004; Rafali & Pratt, 2006; Taylor & Spicer, 2007; Van Marrewijk & Yanow, 2010). Socio-material studies illustrate that the social and the technology material are related in both unidirectional and interactional manners. The exogenous force perspective accounts for technology as a rather autonomous unidirectional driver of organizational change with significant impact on work routines, decision making and governance structures of the organization (see Orlikowski, 2009). From the emergent process and the so-called imbrication perspective, the social human and the technology material are described as interactional. Imbrication, which originally refers to roof tiles (used in ancient Greek and Rome architecture) interlocked by tegula and imbrix for water-proofing a roof, produces the infrastructure of routines and technologies as Leonardi (2011) explains. D'Adderio (2011, p. 198) too focuses on routines, referring to the second wave of research of routines in which agency 'breathes life into routines in a very immediate and intuitive way'. Distinguishing between routine in principle and routine in practice, she develops a framework for examination of the dynamics between routines, agencies and material artefacts.

Studies of the social and the material, described as related spheres of organizational life (Van Marrewijk, 2010), contribute valuable insights into a spatial complexity. Chanlat (2006, p. 18) makes us aware of a spatial complexity, reflected by his definition of organizational space as 'simultaneously divided, controlled, imposed and hierarchical, produc-tive, personalised, symbolic and social'. Scholars inform that physical space affects and structures social interaction (Iedema et al., 2010; Kenis et al., 2010). Descriptions of the physical materiality of space converge with political analyses (cf. Lefebvre, 1991) of production and repro-duction of cultural norms and expectations (Dale & Burrell, 2010) and account for social relations that include asymmetrical relations of power and gender (Panayiotou & Kafiris, 2010). It is shown that organizational space combines organizational design with architectural design (Bellas, 2006; Clegg & Kornberger, 2006; Proffitt Jr & Zahn, 2006) and con-structs meaning and identity (Mobach, 2010).

Engaging with postmodern ideas, scholars stress a becoming aspect of space. Avoiding the fallacy of structure-agency duality thinking (Hernes et al., 2006), they attend to heterotopology in relation to 'thirdspace' which means combining the material and the mental, the real and the imagined (Soja, 1996), and draw attention to transcultural processes (Wåhlin, 2006). Posthumanist perspectives rooted in the principle of symmetry between the human and the non-human are applied with a focus on *sociomateriality* without a hyphen (Gherardi, 2017). Building on Latour's (1987) actor-network theory and Barad's (2003, 2007) work on agential realism influenced by quantum physics, feminist and queer theory, Orlikowski (2007, p. 1437) proposes an entanglement perspective under the assumption that 'there is no social that is not also material, and no material that is not also social'. As expressed by Law and Mol (1995, p. 274) in a more tentative way:

> Perhaps materiality and sociality produce themselves together. Perhaps association is not just a matter for social beings, but also one to do with materials. Perhaps, then, when we look at the social, we are also looking at the production of materiality. And when we look at materials, we are witnessing the production of the social. That, at any rate, is a possibility.

The entanglement perspective accounts for the materiality of technology and directs attention to a fusion of technology and work in the organization with 'space' regarded as one of many socio-material agents (Orlikowki & Scott, 2008). According to the actor-network theory, everything in social and material work exists in constantly shifting networks of relationships (Latour, 2005). As illustrated by heterogeneous socio-technical assemblages (Introna, 2013), hybrid collectives (Chapman et al., 2015) and material-technological network control interlinked with a socio-political dimension (Clegg & Kornberger, 2015), people and technologies are recursively implicated as they use each other to build associations (e.g. Çalişkan & Callon, 2010; Latour, 2005).

The entanglement perspective of sociomateriality shifts the focus away from interactions between the social and the material to intra-actions (Barad, 2003, 2007). Following Barad (2007), Shotter (2014, p. 306) contends that 'not even our bodies can simply take their place in the world ... Rather "environments" and "bodies" are intra-activity co-constituted.' In other words, human beings do not pre-exist and then relate but *become* through intra-action, performatively produced from within a heterogeneous assemblage with appropriations such as tools, gestures, speech, language, communication systems, diet, dress, roles and organization transforming human beings in many unexpected ways (Introna, 2013). However, this implicates that there is 'nothing hiding behind the events through which things interact (or, more felicitously, *intra*-act), nothing behind their phenomenal character and performative articulation', remarks Harman (2016, p. 6, emphasis in original).

As elicited above, a wide range of approaches are suggested to the study of space as it is represented by and also becomes through the social and the material. Organizational spaces provide 'implicit answers to crucial questions of power, order, classification, control and function, while simultaneously implying theories of aesthetics, creativity, innovation and freedom', summarize Clegg and Kornberger (2006, p. 12). There is no universal definition. The complexity of organizational space as elicited by the entanglement perspective rejects any attempt to give answers grounded in a binary assumption that the social and the material are distinct and interdependent spheres of organizational life (Hubbard & Kitchin, 2010; Orlikowski & Scott, 2008; Van Marrewijk, 2010). But, if we rely on an entanglement perspective of sociomateriality that builds on Barad's (2003) conception of intra-action, conceptualizing the human being as performatively produced from within a heterogeneous assemblage, we tend to take the reduction of the human too far (cf. Harman, 2016).

Before opening up to the human as a being-in-the-world, we turn to Taylor and Spicer (2007) for an overview of the highly fragmented literature on the social and the material spheres related to organizational space. Taylor and Spicer (2007) identify three approaches, namely space as distance, space as materialization of power relations and space as lived experience, advocating an integrated spatial approach that accounts for micro, meso and macro levels of the socio-material. This approach gives impetus to a philosophical-oriented discussion that then draws a distinction between space and place, bringing existential and bodily lived spatiality in their material constitution and extension to the fore.

Distance, Power Relations and Lived Experience

The space as distance approach, which also alludes to proximity, directs attention to physical and virtual workplaces, the location of firms, customers and competitors and to the distribution of resources around a building. To exemplify, the geographical location of biotechnical firms depends on access to human resources in the form of 'star scientists' (Almeida & Kogut, 1999). Crucial for financial service firms is access to the reputation of an already existing firm and to sophisticated customers (Pandit & Cook, 2003). Important from a population ecologist perspective is the dynamics of competition (Carroll & Wade, 1991; Sorenson & Audia, 2000), meaning that firms are geographically positioned to attain proximity to competitors rather than to customers (Greve, 2000). From a human ecologist perspective, clusters of firms are mainly driven by interpersonal, regional and interregional relations (Almeida & Kogut, 1999). Regardless of theoretical origin, space as distance is easy to measure; one needs only attend to the physical distance between two points of people, resources or firms, note Taylor and Spicer (2007).

Less measurable, the spatiality of materialization of power relations involves mechanisms for surveillance, control and domination. Communities and company towns built during industrialization with housing provided around factories mobilize such mechanisms. Powerscape and business parks are newer spatial designs conditioned by work organization. The construction of large-scale spaces such as cities, industrial districts, regions and cross-border regions also elucidate materialization of power relations. Workers' identities are regulated through management control to make them comply with organizational goals. Organizational boundaries are extended through the incorporation of the workplace into home and leisure life, leaking organizational norms into non-work space (Taylor & Spicer, 2007).

The space as lived experience approach focuses on 'how spaces are produced and manifest in the experiences of those who inhabit them' (Taylor & Spicer, 2007, p. 333) with time viewed as the most essential part of lived experience (Lefebvre, 1991). Different experiences give rise to different spaces; spaces are shaped by words and stories and can be imbued with poetic and literary images (Bachelard, 1992). Studies framed by organizational symbolism (Gagliardi, 1990) and organizational aesthetics (Strati, 1999) include analyses of cultural and sensory elements of space. A building tells stories about the culture and identity of the organization (Berg & Kreiner, 1990; Yanow, 1998), an organizational space is a space for play (Hjorth, 2005) and an office signifies openness and accountability, exposure and control (Hatch, 1990). The aestheticization of the workplace suggests creating space for play and fun at work. Through reshaped material, cooperation and communication between people are facilitated and 'corridors of power' dismantled (Dale & Burrell, 2010, p. 19).

Organizational Space: An Integrative Approach

As the three organizational space approaches accentuate very different spatial dimensions, Taylor and Spicer (2007) propose an integrative approach to organizational space through drawing on Lefebvre's (1991) theory of the production of space (cf. Hernes, 2004). This theory builds on a conceptual triad, comprising spatial practice, representations of space and representational space. Spatial practice includes production and reproduction to ensure continuity and cohesion, representations of space refers to knowledge, signs and codes, and representational space embraces symbolism (Lefebvre, 1991). The triad is also described in terms of processes of practice, planning and imagining. From the viewpoint of Taylor and Spicer (2007) the process of practice captures space as distance (and proximity), the process of planning corresponds to space as the materialization of power relations, and the imagining process to space as lived experience. This integration helps redefine organizational space as 'practices of distance and proximity which are ordered through planning and interpreted through the ongoing experience of actors' (Taylor & Spicer, 2007, p. 335).

Moreover, the integrative approach accounts for scale of space, which in terms of micro, meso and macro levels of the organization suggests a whole series of hybrid scales and a multiplicity of social spaces that depend on the interest, the mobilization of power and the positioning of actors. The micro scale includes workspace, division of workgroups and gender. The meso scale concerns boundaries 'between the organizational and non-organizational world in points of entry and exit, and spaces of transition such as car parks and lobbies policed by security personnel' (Taylor & Spicer, 2007, p. 337). As Dale and Burrell (2010) comment, community has become a meso level within the organization itself, emphasizing the collective between the state bureaucracy and the free market. 'Corporate social responsibility, stakeholder theory, environmental issues, and "wellness" initiatives all work to give the impression of community involvement and interest', illustrate Dale and Burrell (2010, p. 35). The macro scale attends to the broader geopolitical space including transnational agglomeration and the global economy.

Clearly, the integrative approach links the social with the material but does not devote much interest to the ontological constitution of social and material, space and place. There is limited reflection on lived experience in its hermeneutic-phenomenological singularity with a concern for an ongoing integrative life process through which the individual relates to the Other and to a past (Gadamer, 1989; Heidegger, 1962). In the integrative approach the material is associated with physical properties, disciplinary mechanisms and with a cultural and sensory apparatus that gives rise to plural experiences. Materials are perceived, experienced and used by individuals as they engage in social interactions and activities that take place in and through different organizational spaces, delineated on and across micro, meso and macro levels with little regard to individuals as beings already thrown into the world.

Scholars have begun to draw on Heidegger (1962, 1971) for probing further into the socio-material (e.g. Cecez-Kecmanovic et al., 2014; Chia & Holt, 2006; Ciborra, 2006; Sandberg & Tsoukas, 2011; Schatzki, 2005; Tsoukas, 2015) acknowledging a space that is existential in character. The Heideggerian idea of existential spatiality lends 'unique insights into the development of the sociomaterial practices' (Lamprou, 2017, p. 1736) and helps us break up the totemic conception of space and place. Informed by the philosophical tradition of hermeneutic phenomenology as represented by Heidegger (1962, 1971) the emphasis shifts towards our being-in-the-world, meaning that 'we are so intimately involved with the world that it is not perceived as an object that we apprehend but an extension of us' (Chia, 2004, p. 31). The world is not a container for the individual, the social and the material, or a phenomenon that we can look out upon, but a basic constitution of our being (Elpidorou & Freeman, 2015; Ratcliffe, 2013). Spatiality gains an existential character, understood through the concepts of *Dasein*, mood, care and significance as pointed out next,

EXISTENTIAL SPATIALITY

Existential spatiality is understood through *Dasein* which rejects a subject-object model of worldly existence. Subverting duality-based conceptions of social and material, individual and world, practitioner and practice, actor and activity, *Dasein* accentuates our being in the world, our dwelling, that is, our entwinement with practice in amongst materials. 'Instead of relating to the world primarily by being conscious of it, by representing it, or by intentionally "reaching out" to it, we relate to and are engaged with the world directly and pre-theoretically and on a more primordial level', clarify Elpidorou and Freeman (2015, p. 663). Our engagement implies sharing the world with others. 'By reason of this *with-like* [*mithaften*] Being-in-the-world, the world is always the one that I share with Others. The world of *Dasein* is a *with-world* [*Mitwelt*]. Being-in is *Being-with* Other' (Heidegger, 1962, p. 155, emphasis in original).

'To be a human means to be on the earth as a mortal. It means to *dwell*', says Heidegger (1971, p. 145, emphasis in original). As opposed to 'building', which is premised on productive work that transcribes predesigned forms onto final products and sets the builder over and against the material world, dwelling refers to the ways in which inhabitants carry on their lives through working with and weaving in amongst materials (Ingold, 2011). The building perspective advocates the idea that the builder is a discrete bounded entity, the mental representations of which precede meaningful action (Chia & Rasche, 2015; De La Ville & Mounoud, 2015). As human beings we are not separated from the world, we dwell, entwined with the world. 'Taking entwinement as the primary mode of existence means that for something to be, it needs to show up as something – namely, as part of a meaningful relational totality with other beings', posit Sandberg and Tsoukas (2011, p. 343).

Consistent with the Heideggerian notion of *Dasein* and its adjacent conception of dwelling, entwinement thus entails a non-deliberate mode of engagement in the world, in practice (Chia, 2004; Chia & Holt, 2006). Practice refers to a nexus of activities (Schatzki, 1996) constituted of social interactions and relations, mediating human experience. Materials caught up in these activities define 'a web of functional relationships in which things are encountered with their interdependent functions and relevance to what we are doing' as Gibbs (2008, p. 427) points out. The activities bring the social and the material together. Tsoukas (2015) explains that socio-material activities inscribe an internalized style of practical coping in human agency, performed against a teleological (teleo-affective) structure, an inherited background formed out of habits and customs (Chapter 1). As Schatzki (2010) comments, the activities need not originate in ends specified prior to them, teleologically controlled at a distance. 'Activity is an event, a happening … performing (or doing). Action, by contrast, is *what* happens in the happening that is activity' (Schatzki, 2010, p. xv, emphasis in original) and what is happening is then never fully traceable to preconceived intentions, goals and plans or to a person's values.

Our entwinement with activities and the way in which we encounter material and use material actualize 'mood' and 'care'. Our *Dasein* is disclosed through care in its primordial connection with mood. In conjunction with 'significance', mood and care refer us to a space that is existential in character, aiding our understanding of the happening that is activity.

Dasein Disclosed through Mood and Care

Like atmosphere, mood is already there and we exist in it, disclosing the world to us (Elpidorou & Freeman, 2015). It belongs to and constitutes our *Dasein*, our pre-subjective and pre-objective being-there in the world (Ratcliffe, 2013) and affects and even determines how things appear to us (Elpidorou & Freeman, 2015). Mood comes neither from the outside nor from the inside of a human. It is part of our being-in-the-world and treats affective experience as a fundamental feature of our existence and not as a set of psychic or mental states. Affective mood is not directly related to feelings and emotions as it suggests an ontological relationship with the world, conditioning the possibility of feelings and emotions.

Affective mood discloses the meaningfulness of our existence and is rather understood as *attunement* to a world that is meaningful to us. It is not a generalized emotion or an intentional state but 'a condition of possibility for *intentionality*', foregrounds Ratcliffe (2013, p. 159, emphasis in original). Psychiatric conditions can alter our mood as they are inextricably bound up with our way of being in the world and how we find ourselves in the world (Ratcliffe, 2013). Remote from and prior to cognitive and emotional states mood 'makes manifests "how one is and how one is faring" ["wie einem ist and wird"]. In this "how one is", having a mood brings Being to its "there"', maintains Heidegger (1962, p. 173).

Mood is not the sole determinant of being-in-the-world. Heidegger (1962, p. 215) adds 'care', purporting: 'The care for seeing is essential to man's being.' A few lines of an ancient fable are indicative of how *Dasein* discloses itself as care: 'Once when "Care" was crossing a river, she saw some clay; she thoughtfully took up a piece and began to shape it. While she was meditating on what she had made, Jupiter came by. "Care" asked him to give it spirit ...' (Heidegger, 1962, p. 242). The fable further tells us that Jupiter gave to clay spirit and that Earth gave body, the name of which became *homo* (from *humus*, which means *earth*). Care discloses what we see, conditioned by mood it affects the way in which we encounter and attune with materials and other humans in a world we already are thrown into and share with others. Being-in-the-world is care (*Sorge*), meaning that we encounter the world with others in solicitude – in circumspective concern. 'Letting something be encountered is primarily *circumspective*; it is not just sensing something, or staring at it. It implies circumspective concern, and has the character of being affected in some way', explains Heidegger (1962, p. 176, emphasis in original).

Mood makes circumspective engagement with the world possible. Care in its primordial connection with mood cannot, then, be identified as 'will, wish, addiction, and urge' (Heidegger, 1962, p. 227). We are not separated from the world but part of a meaningful relational totality with other beings, sensitive and responsive to and reflective of emerging circumstances (Schatzki, 2010). Our being-in-the-world, our *Dasein* with affective mood making manifest how we are and how we are faring, has 'the stamp of "care", which accords with its being', according to Heidegger (1962, p. 243). In other words, we are circumspectively engaged with the world, which brings in material things that in their 'equipmentality' construct existential space as they gain theoretical and practical significance in human activity.

Theoretical and Practical Significance

The German word *Zeug* refers to material stuff (things or entities) worked with and used as tools and equipment (a set of tools). Heidegger (1962, p. 97, emphasis in original) explains: 'We shall call those entities which we encounter in concern "*equipment*" ... In our dealings we come across equipment for writing, sewing, working, transportation, measurement.' He adds that there are entities such as leather, hammer, tong and needle used as work equipment in which we discover 'Nature'. Leather is produced by hides taken from animals, and hammer, tong and needle from iron.

In everyday activities we make use of equipment but there is no such thing as 'an equipment', Gibbs (2008, p. 424) accentuates. It is essential to observe that entities in their 'equipmentality' always entail a *Dasein* in the sense of being towards something as an extension of the human and in this is implied existential space with reference to theoretical and practical significance of material things. Implicated in a Heideggerian understanding of socio-material activity is material of theoretical and practical significance (Lamprou, 2017). Materials such as information systems (cf. Lamprou, 2017; Orlikowski & Scott, 2008), pens, knives and saws become tools when effectuated in activity (cf. Ingold, 2011). Prior to their actual use, a possible use is projected, assigning theoretical significance to the material. It is important to observe that theoretical does not mean that equipment is detached from the practice, but that it is 'not (yet) anchored on action' (Lamprou, 2017, p. 1740). Equipment achieves practical significance when actually used in practice. Practical significance refers to how material things come to matter in our activities.

When encountered with new equipment, interruption or breakdown in the use of existing equipment, 'the relational whole of sociomaterial practice is momentarily brought into view' (Sandberg & Tsoukas, 2011, p. 344). In such circumstances there is little connection with established and past ways of practising which certainly requires the practitioner to reflect carefully on theoretical significance assigned the equipment. When tensions emerge between theoretical and practical significance there is the need for revisiting theoretical significance, reflecting on how information is provided about material and in what mood the individuals find themselves when encountered with the material.

Theoretical and practical significance pertains to a space that resists physical extendedness. In relation to Heideggerian significance, a spatial feature such as proximity (or distance) is a feature that responds to the question of how far or near the material is for acquiring significance in practice (Schatzki, 2010). Physical proximity to and available use of material do not explain how the material interweaves with the social as we need to account for our being-in-the-world and the way in which we find ourselves when encountering material and becoming attuned to it. Material in the functionality of equipment is there along with us, caught up in our activities – in care conditioned by affective mood. The distinction made between theoretical and practical significance thus reflects differences in people's ways of being as their *Daseins* are disclosed by mood and care. Material interweaves with the social as a being-in-the-world human contemplates the use of materials and actually uses materials. With the move from theoretical to practical significance then space extends in an existential sense. This move could be thought of as a heterogeneous assemblage, a process through which the individual becomes as the individual extends through equipment utilized, achieving certain accomplishments (cf. Introna, 2013). In appropriating a pen, for example, the individual becomes a being who can write, which is something else than an individual without a pen and a pen without an individual. For Heidegger (1962) tools create works or products that are extensions of the self (Casey, 2001).

It is important to note that hermeneutic phenomenology emphasizes interpretation and understanding of our being in the world. In opposition to Edmund Husserl's (1859–1936) phenomenology, defined as the study of the things in themselves, which essence belongs to consciousness described by transcendental subjectivity, Heidegger (1962) pursues the idea that being is historical and temporal and lies beyond every 'thing'. In other words, interpretation and understanding aim at a priori conditions. Our being in the world cannot be broken up in pieces and then put together. Phenomenology becomes hermeneutic through exceeding *essential* treatment of things. Things *in* our world are encountered, in circumspection defined by the present-at-hand and the ready-to-hand.

Hermeneutic phenomenology belongs to things in terms of their presence and readiness at hand.

The Heideggerian notion of dwelling as understood in terms of a human's entwinement with activity is also included in geographical and anthropological work. Dwelling and its adjacent notion of entwinement claims landscape, conveyed as *place* and a world of materials that is *with* us and bodily lived in the present. This present calls on a past that tells about how our predecessors *scaped* land. By giving primacy to move-ment we further recognize that people are not contained within a place as merely dwellers but carry on as 'wayfarers'.

PLACE AS *SCAPED* LAND

Geographical work has increasingly engaged with hermeneutic-phenomenological work and a clear distinction has been made between space and place. 'The intrinsic difference between space and place is nowhere more evident than in the role of a primary feature of landscape, its *horizon*. Every landscape has a horizon, yet space never does', high-lights Casey (2001, p. 690, emphasis in original). There is no landscape of space but of place, 'constituted as an enduring record of – and testimony to – the lives and works of past generations who have dwelt within it, and in so doing, have left there something of themselves', submits Ingold (1993, p. 152). Landscape as *place* has a horizon, and is something more than a spot traced on a cartographic map and a spot traversed by a tourist. It is 'scaped' by the human body.

Ingold (2011, p. 126) reminds us that the suffix 'scape' attached to 'land' comes from the old English word *sceppan* (or *skyppan*), which means 'to shape'. The medieval shapers were farmers, scaping the land 'with foot, axe and plough, and with the assistance of their domestic animals trod, hacked and scratched their lines into the earth, and thereby created its ever-evolving texture ... in an immediate, muscular and visceral engagement with wood, grass and soil' (Ingold, 2011, p. 126). Scaped, place is bodily lived, enfolding the lines of people who have reached out and have come in to it and have become 'placilized'.

Placilizing the Human Body

Bridging geographical work and hermeneutic-phenomenological work, Casey (2001) points to experiential features of place. The human being is a geographical self that orients to a place, reaches out to it and when coming in to it becomes placilized and a bearer of idiolocality. Following Bourdieu (1977), the concepts of habitus and habitation are used to explain the mediatrix of place and the bodily self. Habitus is the basis of human action and refers to the self's experiences in place and the re-enactment of the experiences, the customs and norms developed over time. Habitation is the active commitment to place that could include both nomadic movement and settled dwelling, according to Casey (2001). Habitation is distinguished from occupation since there is no ready-made world for the inhabitant to occupy but a world that develops, extends and regenerates through inhabitants' activities. Casey (2001), borrowing the term 'thirdspace' from Soja (1996), calls this world a place-world.

Soja (1996) launches the thirdspace logic. It is attributed two meanings: 'the first arising from an ontological argument about the co-equal privileging of the spatial, the historical, and the social; the second derived from a critique of the binary logic that has dominated traditional ways of thinking about space and geography for at least the past century' (Soja, 1996, p. 114).

While habitus and habitation do not explain the specificity and persistence of place in our body, Casey (2001) sees it necessary to include the notions of tenacity, subjection and idiolocality. Tenacity concerns our intense experiences of a place, and subjection the way in which a place becomes part of us. Coming in to a place implies placilizing the human body, which also means becoming a bearer of idiolocality, being subjected to a place in its idiosyncrasies. The body 'is shaped by the places it has come to know and that have come to it' (Casey, 2001, p. 688). Multisensory experience of place, visual, aural and tactile provide means by which place is evoked.

Since materials are mixed and transformed continually by the inhabitants we must put more emphasis on movement. With a focus on place-binding, Ingold (2011) takes an anthropological approach to place that relates to Heidegger's (1971) dwelling, but as opposed to Heidegger (1971), who draws a sharp line between animals, captivated in their *Umwelt*, and human beings, Ingold sees the world opens up to both humans and non-humans including animals.

Place-Binding and Wayfaring

Without making a sharp distinction between humans and other living organisms, Ingold (2011) makes ecology an equivalent ontology to the Heideggerian being-in-the-world ontology. Inspired by Deleuze and

Guattari (2004), he views the living organism as a bundle of lines, also described as a fungal mycelium. Place is then a world of materials under continuous construction – a meshwork of lifelines:

> In such a world, persons and things do not so much exist as occur, and are identified not by any fixed, essential attributes laid down in advance or transmitted ready-made from the past, but by the very paths (or trajectories, or stories) along which they have previously come and presently going. (Ingold, 2011, p. 141)

Materials are things encountered in the land *scaped* by people, including various forms of animals, plants, fugal and bacterial life, and things transformed by human activity into artefacts. The ground is 'a textured composite of diverse materials that are grown, deposited and woven together through a dynamic interplay' (Ingold, 2011, p. 130), which accords well with the etymological definition of material as 'mother', disclosed as the active constituent of a world-in-formation (see Chapter 1).

A manifold of forms arise as human and non-human constituents thread their ways and these forms are held in place, not in space. To be held in place does not exclude movement. Ingold (2011) uses the term 'place-binding' to maintain that humans do not live their lives inside a place (place-bound) but through, around, to and from it. This makes them wayfarers; place-binding implicates wayfaring. By borrowing the term 'meshwork' from Lefebvre (1991), Ingold (2011) accentuates the texture of life. Place is not furnished with objects and ready to be occupied but a world under continuous construction, a meshwork of lifelines in which we are not bound but subjected to binding in its sense of wayfaring. To participate in a world is to be along lines (or paths). As wayfarers inhabitants proceed along lines and where lines meet, *knots* are identified. Ingold (2011, p. 149, emphasis in original) explains:

> Places, then, are like knots, and the threads from which they are tied are lines of wayfaring. A house, for example, is a place where the lines of its residents are tightly knotted together. But these lines are no more contained within the house than are threads contained within a knot. Rather, they trail beyond it, only to become caught up with other lines in other places, as are threads in other knots. Together they make up what I have called the *meshwork*.

When looking to 'place' as a piece of a landscape and a world of materials we thus realize that the social and the material, the human and the non-human including animals, come together in the form of a meshwork.

It is predicated on the idea that 'beings do not simply occupy the world, they *inhabit* it, and in so doing – in threading their own paths through the meshwork – they contribute to its evolving weave' (Ingold, 2011, p. 71, emphasis in original). Rather than routing across a place from point to point, the inhabitants as wayfarers thread their paths through, around, to and from a place. Place is 'a tangled mesh of interwoven and complexly knotted strands' (Ingold, 2011, p. 151). It opens up to bodily experiential explorations (cf. Lefebvre, 1991). The abstractness of space discourages experiential exploration; the 'enactive vehicle of being-in-place is the *body*', insists Casey (2001, p. 687, emphasis in original).

IN SUMMATION

As pointed out in this chapter, social and material, space and place are dimensions of organizational life dealt with in studies applying unidirectional, interactional, political, gender, architectural, thirdspace, transcultural, actor-network and entanglement perspectives. In spite of a rich variety of socio-material studies there is limited concern for family business. Also the three broad socio-material approaches presented in the chapter dedicate little interest to family business organizational life. Space as distance, space as materialization of power relations and space as lived experience, and the integration of these conceptions of space, afford insights into the social in conjunction with the material without including family business.

To probe deeper into the issue of space and place the chapter refers to studies informed by the philosophical tradition of hermeneutic phenomenology. It reveals that scholars taking an interest in the social and the material have begun to draw on Heidegger's (1962, 1971) philosophy with *Dasein* designating a human's way of being in the world. This includes dwelling, which in association with entwinement refers to the ways in which humans carry on their lives, engaging in activity, immersed in materials. Space extends through the ways in which material is appropriated in activities. By specifically pointing to existential spatiality as care, a dynamic lens for studying socio-material activity is provided. Care in its primordial connection with affective mood makes us aware of a space that extends as people change their ways of being through activities caught up with materials ascribed theoretical and practical significance.

A hermeneutic-phenomenological perspective, applied in geographical (Casey, 2001) and anthropological work (Ingold, 2011), provides us with another dynamic lens for studying socio-material activity. As noted, place is bodily lived and this suggests a focus on placilizing, place-binding and a meshwork of lifelines. Place-binding entails that humans in a bodily sense live their lives through, around, to and from a place. Inhabitants are wayfarers who proceed along paths threaded by people not living any longer, connecting with them while also deviating from them. Place is a world of materials under continuous construction – a meshwork of lines with houses described as knots of residents' lifelines.

How to make present 'family business' as socio-material weaving in the account of space and place is a methodological question that must reflect a hermeneutic-phenomenological awareness that family business is not 'there' but extends through activities and further, that genuinely related individuals (Chapter 1) are beings-in-the-world with others, and that materials in their serviceability as tools are reflective of a *Dasein* being, present-at-hand and ready-to-hand when ascribed theoretical and practical significance. The ensuing chapter brings in narrative and story, eliciting that it is through written and spoken words a *Dasein* existence is communicated. It introduces a being-in-the-world narrative methodology that points us in the direction of an understanding, intimately connected with interpretation, of empirical-oriented information interlaced with theory concerned with the social and the material and with space and place.

4. Narrative and story and a being-in-the-world methodology

Narrative and story appeal to our senses, reason and emotion, intellect and imagination (cf. Fisher, 1984) and are expressed in numerous ways. 'Among the vehicles of narrative are articulated language, whether oral or written, pictures, still or moving, gestures ... narrative is present in myth, legend, fables, tales ... stained glass windows, movies, local news, conversation', reveal Barthes and Duisit (1975, p. 237). Narrative approaches are adopted in studies of organization, entrepreneurship, management and geography and in recent years, studies of family and family business. As Richardson (2000, p. 168) summarizes: 'Now, narrative is everywhere.' Yet, little is known about business activity narratives that in the form of stories, carried by written and spoken words, account for people as storytelling beings-in-the-world.

The chapter begins with a note on poetry and literature and continues with a discussion on family and family business narratives and stories. With reference to Ricoeur (1992) and Heidegger (1962) it suggests a being-in-the-world narrative methodology, which implies a qualitative method that accentuates interpretation and understanding of people's stories about activities and materials. A distinction is made between narrative and story. As pointed out, intelligibility of being-in-the world expresses itself as discourse, language broken up in words constitutive of stories. The being-in-the-world narrative methodology introduces the storytelling animal, *homo narrans*, who in written and spoken words communicates a *Dasein* existence.

The chapter also includes a description of the generation of empirical-oriented information and the collaborative interaction process through which stories emerge between the storyteller and the researcher (Fivush et al., 2004). It emphasizes that interpretation and understanding occur in an ongoing fashion, directed by philosophical-theoretical considerations about existential space and bodily lived place for the development of theory and a narrative truth.

IN POETRY AND LITERATURE THEORY

Ancient Greek writing directs our attention to poetry, defined as 'the organization of incidents in drama, guided by art (*technē*) to form a plot' (Hutton, 2018, p. 48). According to Aristotle (384–322 bc) plot is the soul of a form of poetry called tragedy and is likened to 'the chalk drawing an artist sketches before filling it in with colour and to a creature that is organically whole' (in Hutton, 2018, p. xxiii). 'Plot' corresponds to the Greek word 'mythos', which means 'story', and is usually recognized by its cohesive beginning, middle and end (Hutton, 2018). Aristotle uses the term plot to imitate actions and life, urging the poet, whether a man of genius or one having a touch of madness, to construct plot by means of a language that places the emphasis on action (*praxis*). Narrative is a form of language spoken by the poet in the third person; a language spoken by characters in their own voice is called dramatic speech (Hutton, 2018). Already, the Aristotelian early form of narration makes us aware of the relation between story and discourse.

More than two thousand years later, in the 1960s, a narrative turn began in literary theory, and as Hyvärinen (2010, p. 72) informs, this turn suggested 'the institutional study of narrative for its own sake'. Narrative had always been part of literature studies but was now presented as an autonomous object of inquiry with structuralist linguistics as a basis of scientific narratology.

> The underlying assumption was that the structure of a narrative resembles the structure of other linguistic expressions and that the code in which a message is communicated can be identified and separated from the content of the message. Structuralists believe in a closed grammatical system based on rationally ordered functional units. They are advocators of the view that language using this structure helps divide the world into stable units. (Ericson, 2010, p. 7)

Russian structuralists paid attention to the archetypal type of fairy tales (Polkinghorne, 1988). On the basis of biographical and chronological perspectives French structuralists prioritized determinism and objectivity in the historical study of literature and society (Weimann, 1973). Focus centred also on the relationship between history and literature with regard to 'techniques, rules, rituals and collective mentality' (Weimann, 1973, p. 441). Without reference to history, American structuralists advocated 'new criticism' (Polkinghorne, 1988), treating the literary text of poetry, drama and novel as an autonomous whole (see also Ericson, 2010).

In the wake of structuralist linguistics, narrative approaches evolved to highlight the narrator, reader, listener and the user of a text. From postmodern perspectives scholars point to 'ongoing dynamic texts constructed in an infinite number of ways by readers or listeners rather than storytellers' (Cunliffe et al., 2004, p. 264). The postmodernist sees language as a tool for reality construction, a construction that is never finished (Czarniawska, 2004). With reference to an artificial intelligence community, virtual reality is approached as a narrative medium with narrative depicted as a 'storification' process resulting from interactions between the characters and the users (Aylett & Louchart, 2003). Digital narratives permit a close relationship between the public (the readers) and the producers (Grafström & Lid Falkman, 2017). 'Any story, any form of rhetorical communication, not only says something about the world, it also implies an audience, persons who conceive of themselves in very specific ways', comments Fisher (1984, p. 14).

Literature theory has spread in humanities and social sciences (e.g. Boje, 1991; Boje et al., 1999; Brown & Rhodes, 2005; Czarniawska, 1997, 2004) and has also inspired family and family business scholars to adopt narrative approaches, often using 'story' and 'narrative' interchangeably.

IN STUDIES OF FAMILY

In studies of family, stories serve as 'method, medium and meaning' summarize Fiese and Pratt (2004, p. 413). Stories extend along the life cycle, from childhood to old age and across generations (Pratt & Fiese, 2004). Depending on family complexity, described by the number of family members and their relationships, and the number of living generations (Gimeno Sandig et al., 2006), multiple stories emerge. From a developmentalist perspective Pratt and Fiese (2004, p. 2) present narrative as 'a way of thinking and knowing, and as a core element in the individual's growth and change across the life course'. It is contended that narratives in the form of personal life stories aid our understanding of how the inner self relates to outer behaviours. The developmentalist perspective is grounded in a systems view with the family depicted as a system (a 'whole') that consists of members that affect and are affected by the family and where both the family and the individual are ascribed inner and outer features. In this system there are overlapping sets of dyadic relationships, for example, parent and child, husband and wife.

Through stories family members connect across generations as presented by a narrative ecology of family life. As McAdams (2004, p. 235) illustrates: 'Two partners have a story about how they met ... They each have stories about their own families ... Their parents and siblings have their stories ... and on it goes.' The stories afford generativity in that they allow values and moral messages to be passed down from one generation to another, and destructive practices or beliefs to be blocked by a family for instilling new hope for the future generation. A story 'contains a setting within which action makes sense, an actor whose intentions are translated into goal-directed behaviour, and an ending through which the emotional tension created by the story's events is resolved or dismissed', according to McAdams (2004, p. 237).

Implicit in family stories are 'messages for both socialization and relationship values' as Fiese and Pratt (2004, p. 410) point out, conceiving of family stories as conveyors of culture for developing the child as the child grows into adolescence. By spending much time with their children, parents greatly influence the narrative skills of the children (Peterson & McCabe, 2004). Dickstein (2004) conceptualizes marriage as an attachment construct, an intimate adult relationship embedded within the family system, with implications for the child–parent relationship. It is assumed that the child–parent relationship is the most enduring bond of family relationships (Pratt & Fiese, 2004), and that marital attachment has a profound impact on the child's sense of self and expectations of emotional and social support (Dickstein, 2004).

Further, developmentalists focus their attention on tracing lexical and grammatical use of language in the narrative discourse. Aksu-Koç and Aktan-Erciyes (2018) studied children's narrative production during their preschool and early school years. The activity of production implies forwarding a plot that informs about the actor(s), where and when actions take place, and the intentionality behind the actions. This narrative rests on a skilful use of linguistic forms that contributes a coherent narrative and provides communicative adequacy through which comprehension by the audience is ensured.

As elicited, narratives in the form of family stories serve as a medium for transferring information, values and morals between members of the family and across generations. Stories promote the making of meaning and the construction of a sense of identity for the individual member and the family. Narrative suggests a linguistic device for a coherent configuration of the plot of a story. The family constitutes a system in which ecological levels and dyadic relationships between members of the family are identified with little concern for socio-material weaving.

IN STUDIES OF FAMILY BUSINESS

In studies of family business we note the influence of business history research (Chapter 2) and the use of inductive narratives and cases (Holt & Popp, 2013). Family business scholars have not been very receptive to narrative approaches (Dawson & Hjorth, 2011). Their studies have been dominated by quantitative methods (Nordqvist et al., 2009), but narrative approaches are beginning to appear in family business research. In extension to qualitative-interpretive methodologies, narratives, stories and storytelling (Smith, 2018) give insights into the social dynamic and relational qualities of human interaction and processes over generations (Dawson & Hjorth, 2011). According to Smith (2018, pp. 41–2), it is important to distinguish between narrative and story: 'A story is a narration of events containing basic features such as setting, plot, characters, and a sequence of events in a logical manner with a beginning, middle and an end. A narrative is an overarching organisational structure designed to facilitate the recounting of sequential events and experiences'.

Smith (2018) points to luminal space, meaning that stories about entrepreneurship and family business interweave (cf. Kar & Samantarai, 2011) since the familiar and the entrepreneurial are dual worlds. In analysing this duality, Smith (2018) uses data, the bulk of which is accessed via the Internet, illustrating how the public-narrative of a family business is constructed as a business saga for public consumption. 'The public-narrative traces the epic rise of the family, narrating real-life romances and adventures of couples in love with each other and business' (Smith, 2018, p. 52).

The importance of expanding our theoretical understanding of narrative, stories and storytelling is increasingly acknowledged (Jaskiewicz et al., 2015; Kammerlander et al., 2015; Smith, 2018). From the viewpoint of Hamilton et al. (2017, p. 7), 'Every family business represents a context in which family narratives may exist in tandem with business objectives and goals.' Narratives help 'family scholars recognize that human cognition and emotion are fundamentally wedded to story', purports Harrison (2014, p. 113).

Family and business, conceived of as interacting systems, provide a context for storytelling (Smith, 2018). Devoid of a material aspect it is a context that gives prominence to a social aspect. Through a longitudinal case study Parada and Viladás (2010) organize empirical data in the form of narratives that serve as social vehicles for sensemaking, transmission of values across generations, and construction of identity in family businesses. 'By telling stories, family businesses are able to build identity and shared meanings which led to successful performance in terms of revenues, reputation, shared identity, and continuity of the family business history', conclude Parada and Viladás (2010, p. 166).

In addition, Parada and Dawson (2017) explain how family businesses build their collective identity through trans-generational stories from individual identity construction, with case study material based on interviews presented in the form of narratives. On the basis of a case study, Kar and Samantarai (2011) present stories that convey information about a family business embedded in a value system sustained by networks of kinship and friendship formed around an ethnic community. Addressing the succession process in a family business, Dawson and Hjorth (2011) employ a narrative approach that draws on the autobiography of the owner and manager of a family business and contribute insight into the complexity of a father–son relationship. Autobiographies are a literary genre that builds on life stories. Dawson and Hjorth's (2011) autobiographical narrative approach deals with the social dynamics performed in language-use, providing intimate connection with empirical realities.

Informed by Ricoeur's Philosophical Work

It is particularly interesting to note that Hamilton (2006) adopts a narrative approach that originates in Ricoeur's (e.g. 1984) philosophical work on narrative. She makes use of Aristotle's emplotment elements of reversal, recognition and suffering for an interpretation of the founding of a family business and its transformation to the next generation. In her study, emplotment is a configuration and reconfiguration process that endows experience with meaning. Reversal concerns the decision of the first generation to start a business and the decision of the second generation to join, recognition is associated with entrepreneurial learning, and suffering accounts for dramatic events such as sudden illnesses. For Aristotle (Hutton, 2018), the actions of the agent in the tragedy could imply reversal, recognition and suffering with reversal being a change from one state to an opposite state, recognition a change from ignorance to knowledge, and suffering adhering to destruction and physical pain that render pity and fear. Aristotle devotes more attention to recognition than to reversal with plot disclosing how the agent reaches an understanding of error and evil that emanate from the agent's doings towards others, morally enlightened and relieved (Hutton, 2018).

Hamilton (2006, p. 538) emphasizes the pre-narrative capacity of life, meaning that the 'we have to look for points of support for narrative in the experience of the mixture of acting and suffering which make up the fabric of life, and what in that experience demands the assistance of narrative'. We draw on narratives that already are available to us as part of our culture, aware that suffering is an enduring element of our life.

The Ricoeurian narrative is informed by a hermeneutic phenomenology that presumes a human's being in the world and a dialogical openness to the Other. In the mixture of acting and suffering the individual self might then not be able to uphold sameness in terms of character and traits, but changes, temporalized and actualized in relation to the Other (see Ericson & Kjellander, 2018). From the viewpoint of Ricoeur (1992) then, narrative does not presuppose a linear plot based on a causal-type model of occurrences with a beginning, middle and an end. Leaving plot aside and requirements of a temporal linearity that causally links event to event, stories suspend time-sequence, coherence and closure (Boje, 2000).

Ricoeur's (1992) notion of the pre-narrative has a certain affinity with Heidegger's (1962) notion of *Dasein*. For the development of an alternative approach to the study of family business, narrative and *Dasein* are not merely of ontological interest but also methodological.

A BEING-IN-THE-WORLD METHODLOGY

There are hermeneutic-phenomenological parallels between Ricoeur's (1992) conception of narrative and Heidegger's (1962) conception of *Dasein*, our being-in-the-world. The world is not an object to which the self subject relates, posits Heidegger (1962), in agreement with whom Ricoeur (1992, p. 313) expresses: 'The fact that the self and being-in-the-world are basic correlates seems indisputable to me.' Being in the world, pre-narratively engaged, entails a move in between present actualities and future possibilities, and also acknowledges a past as a historicizing process and a 'having-been-there' (Heidegger, 1962).

Although narrative is not explicitly addressed by Heidegger (1962), the conception of *Dasein* amounts to a narrative conception of the self, asserts Roth (2018). *Dasein* signifies that we should not take ourselves as something present-at-hand at a given moment as we ourselves are our possibilities; *Dasein* refers to our existence in between present actualities and future possibilities, implicating a narrative structure of being-in-the-world (Roth, 2018). Our future orientation emphasizes the unfinished nature of *Dasein* and this is precisely what elucidates our narrativity, according to Roth (2018, p. 752), because 'the unfinished parts of ourselves are filled in by projected narrative ... just as we read narratives before knowing how they end, we read ourselves in an open-ended fashion, in light of possibilities that may or may not unify our lives into purposive wholes'.

When turning our sight towards a past we also realize that there is no one single plot to follow. As Riessman (1993, p. 6) points out: 'Narratives do not mirror ... The "truths" of narrative accounts are not in their faithful representations of a past world, but in the shifting connections they forge among past, present and future.' As in a meshwork of lifelines (Ingold, 2011) there is no single path along which the history of business activities unfolds. 'Depending on where we are now, and what we are considering, we will see different parts of our pasts' (Roth, 2018, p. 753). We might refer to events occurring over vast periods of time or within a brief period (Gergen & Gergen, 1997). A conception of history entails a historcizing process that stretches along *Dasein* and along which *Dasein* is stretched (Heidegger, 1962). As Gadamer (1989), a student of Heidegger, adds, history is a living (cultural) tradition that shapes our present and future. As social historical beings we are always affected by and bound to the testimony of history. Belongingness to the world makes tradition a 'partner' with which we can enter into a dialogue (cf. Ericson, 2007, 2010).

As indicated, being-in-the-world can be ascribed a narrative structure. Narrative then does not only serve as a vehicle for transmitting information, values and morals, constructing meaning and identity (Fiese & Pratt, 2004) and as a method for accessing and analysing data (De Fina, 2009; Smith, 2018). Narrative is central to our existence as in Ricoeur's (1992) hermeneutic phenomenology of narrative with reference to the pre-narrative. 'We author our lives. We narrate our lives' (Roth, 2018, p. 746). As MacIntyre (1981, p. 216) expresses it: 'A central thesis then begins to emerge: man is in his actions and practice, as well as in his fictions, essentially a story-telling animal.'

Homo Narrans and the Use of Language

As a storytelling animal, *homo narrans* (Fisher, 1984), we use language. Since intelligibility of being-in-the world expresses itself as discourse and discourse is language broken up in words (Heidegger, 1962), it is through language that stories unfold. Language then is not a mere means in a communication process. Drawing on Cunliffe (2002), Helin (2011, p. 57) underlines, 'it is in language, in the conversations themselves, that social worlds are created'. We cannot neglect the notion of language as the universal medium through which we live our lives. In the words of Shotter (2003, p. 444, emphasis in the original), world and language are 'all *internally* related participant parts of a larger, indivisible, dynamic whole, a ceaseless stream of ongoing activity, of understandable-being in motion'.

The being-in-the-world narrative methodology involves *homo narrans*, who in written and spoken words communicates a *Dasein* existence. Hence, it presumes a move in between present actualities and future possibilities with historicizing occurring along *Dasein* with the past referred to as a having-been-there and as a communicative partner. The methodology allows for different temporal orientations and multiple plots to play out. The storyteller might refer to events occurring over vast periods of time or within a brief period (Gergen & Gergen, 1997). When linking Ricoeur's (1992) conception of narrative, we realize that human interactions and relations allow for change and fragmentation of life plot. Along *Dasein* – in a meshwork of lifelines – it is difficult to form a coherent story. Beginnings, middles and ends are preliminary because the storyteller can never stand outside of her life and grasp it as a whole.

The being-in-the-world narrative methodology presupposes a qualitative method that accentuates interpretation and understanding of empirical-oriented information, in this book generated through numerous visits to Tällberg and meetings with Tällberg inhabitants involved in business activities. The term 'empirical-oriented' is used to indicate that there is no data 'out there' to be collected, no pure empirics or facts to detect (Alvesson & Kärreman, 2007).

Generation of Empirical-Oriented Information

In 2016, I met with the President and the Vice President of the local heritage society in Tällberg. They provided an overview of business developments and family-owned hotel businesses and presented me with a book of more detailed descriptions of the transformation of Tällberg from a farmer village to a tourist village. To get a feel for what it is like to bodily live and move around in the Tällberg place material I rented a cottage for a couple of months in the autumn of 2017. In accordance with a philosophical tradition of hermeneutic phenomenology the human is a 'knowing body' (Casey, 1993, p. 52). The human body and its moves through a place is 'a medium through which to articulate provisional understandings' of that place (Van Marrewijk & Yanow, 2010, p. 7). Very often I visited the library in the neighbouring village of Leksand, generating information from books about life in Dalarna and Tällberg, nature and culture, the old family tradition which meant that several generations including grandparents and grandchildren lived under the same roof, the long walks undertaken by people to find work elsewhere in times when crop production at the family farm failed, and about the shipping of people and goods on Lake Siljan.

During 2018, I visited all eight hotels in Tällberg (Delacarlia, Green Hotel, Gyllene Hornet, Hotel Siljanstrand, Klockargården, Tällbergsgården, Villa Långbers and Åkerblads) meeting with the receptionists to obtain some general information about the hotels and the current ownership. Hotel-specific brochures and web pages provided additional information. When initiating the study I decided it would be particularly interesting to include Siljanstrand, Green Hotel, Klockargården, Tällbergsgården and Åkerblads which in terms of business activities involved families, the Börjeson, the Alm, the Sandberg and the Åkerblad families. The Siljanstrand and the Green Hotel story revolve around first-generation family owning activities. Siljanstrand is strongly associated with Hans Erik Börjeson and with a past that refers to Siljansgården, stretching back to the beginning of the twentieth century and it makes present the guest home lodging and educational activities of the three-generation Alm family. The Börjeson family also draws our attention to Green Hotel. Klockargården introduces the five-generation Sandberg family and provides glimpses of a variety of business activities in the chronology of time covering more than nine decades. Tällbergsgården and Åkerblads present the Åkerblad family with the youngest family members representing the 22nd generation. Members of the mentioned families and others with whom genuine relationships are maintained (Chapter 1) tell about 'family business', not as something separated from their lives, but as something that is made present in a flow of activities, constituted of their interactions and relations in amongst materials. In the words uttered, the social and the material are brought together.

In between 'story partners'

The study intensified during a three-year period from spring 2018 to spring 2021. Through face-to-face meetings and documentary information about Tällberg and the hotels, including books, articles, web pages and hotel brochures, stories evolved. My first contact was with the owners of the hotels; 'ownership' serves as the preliminary starting point for the stories. At the initiation of the study, ownership is attributed a legal relationship with the hotel conceived of as a legal entity. By applying a perspective that translates ownership into activities we are able to move beyond such reification. The meetings with the hotel owners indicated that they were 'involved in everything' and that 'ownership' dissolved into owning activities performed in close relation to activities with which others entwine. People holding formal positions such as CEO, hotel manager, marketing manager and head of household also described what they were doing in interaction with others.

The face-to-face meetings were broadly introduced through a description of the research project and its focus on family business as activities performed in Tällberg. The opening of the meetings provided a loose structure to encourage people to tell about activities and their relations to Tällberg in the way they found comfortable and relevant (cf. Fivush et al., 2004). On account of the book's fascination for a place called Tällberg, activities that engaged material related to other places that Hans Erik Börjeson, the Alm, the Sandberg and the Åkerblad families visited, experienced and dwelled in during different periods of their lives, were excluded.

Through collaborative interaction stories emerged (Fivush et al., 2004). The researcher is not an interviewer or observer, rather a 'story partner' acting as a mediator, in interaction with others facilitating storytelling. As a story partner I followed the curves and turns, anfractuous in character the stories did not take a straight path linearly unfolding in time. Small comments were inserted to express my interest in what was being told and to encourage the person to tell about the present position and what the position meant in terms of activities, interactions and relations with members of the family and others, what materials the person was encountered with and used with activities, and further, what the person associated with 'Tällberg' and considered important to care for at present with sights on the future. I also engaged in 'polite turn-taking', a term used by Fivush et al. (2004), to promote elaboration on activities performed and situations experienced, carefully listening to the words uttered and not dominating the exchange. The stories do not unfold through questions and answers as in a traditional interview. The relevance of the stories arises out of the story partners' interaction (cf. Rae, 2005).

At the second meeting with some of the genuinely related individuals I provided a summary of the previous meeting. The exchange between story partners present at the second meeting made it possible to re-enter utterances made during the first meeting and ask for more details on activities, interactions and relations and materials. Also feelings felt when encumbered with sorrows and faced with burn-out and other challenges were shared with me at these meetings.

Thirty-three face-to-face meetings with 19 genuinely related individuals, eight hotel receptionists and two artists ranged from 15 to 120 minutes, excluding guided tours indoors and outdoors. The meetings took place in a coffee room, a conference room in the main hotel building, the owner's home, at the reception desk, in a room for an art exhibition and in a café in the nearby village of Leksand. Via nine telephone meetings people told me about their doings, materials used and what Tällberg means to them. Fourteen emails contributed pieces of information about hotel business activities in relation to Tällberg. The face-to-face meetings were tape recorded and transcribed by me verbatim. Notes were taken during the telephone meetings. All information, including email and text presented on the Internet about the hotels, in brochures and in books, was provided in Swedish and translated by me into English. With reference to Gadamer (1989) I have explained elsewhere (Ericson, 2018, p. 11) that one must be 'cautious about the translation of the meaning understood in one context to another context. This requires an interpretation that bridges a gap between the original words and the reproduced words and awareness that the translation cannot remove the fundamental gap between two languages'.

The owner of Siljanstrand, Hans Erik Börjeson, died in July 2020, and there was no opportunity given him to read the final version of the chapter including the Siljanstrand and the Green Hotel story and to consent to publishing the parts quoting him. Therefore, those stories build solely on official documentary text, including text presented in a book written by Börjeson, translated by me into English. The wife of the former owner of Klockargården died in March 2020. The owner consented to publishing the Klockargården story text that cited his wife. All other persons included in the stories have given me the permission to publish the stories and use their full names.

Understanding: The Explicit Form of Interpretation

In understanding 'lurks the possibility of interpretation – that is, of appropriating what is understood', posits Heidegger (1962, p. 203). Understanding is interrelated with interpretation and occurs through language such that our horizons are enlarged and enriched (Gadamer, 1989). As pointed out elsewhere (e.g. Ericson & Melin, 2010) with reference to Gadamer (1989, p. 302): 'The horizon is the range of vision that includes everything that can be seen from a particular vantage point.' It is thus in dialogue with the Other we are able to come to an understanding (Ericson, 2018) and in this book, with reference to 'story partners'. Not losing hermeneutic-phenomenological sight the researcher must remember that she too is a storyteller, thrown into the world in togetherness with the other *homo narrans*. There is no subject-object relationality that separates the investigated object and the researcher as investigator since they both orient to each other and mutually adjust. In relational responsiveness to each other (Fletcher, 2007) the story partners advance their understanding through a fusion of horizons (Gadamer, 1989).

Understanding as the explicit form of interpretation occurs in an ongoing fashion of information generated during face-to-face meetings, via telephone calls and emails. It is informed by research literature related to three areas, family business, social and material, space and place, and text focused on Tällberg, its inhabitants, hotels, guest home and school. Philosophical-theoretical considerations *direct* our understanding, making us pay particular attention to business-oriented activities caught up in materials that relate to spatiality as expressed in terms of existential space and bodily lived place. The hermeneutic-phenomenological concepts of *Dasein*, mood, care, circumspection and significance (Ciborra, 2006; Elpidorou & Freeman, 2015; Gibbs, 2008; Heidegger, 1962; Lamprou, 2017) direct us to existential space, and the geography- and anthropology-related concepts of tenacity and subjection, concerned with the placilizing of the human body (Casey, 2001), and the concept of landscape with reference to a shaped land (Ingold, 2011), direct us to bodily lived place. Through a focus on people's entwinement with activities, being observant on the ways in which the activities are caught up with materials, understanding implies concerned contact with family business as an emergent phenomenon. Less interested in *analysis* of a business system mutually related to a family system located in an external environment, the being-in-the-world narrative methodology, suggested in this chapter, enables a philosophical-theoretical-empirical *understanding* that inspires the development of a social-material weaving theory and a narrative truth, elaborated in the concluding chapter (Chapter 8).

Qualitative method literature supplies little information on 'weaving'. In connection with textile fabrics 'weaving' is an activity in which two sets of threads are used, the warp and the weft that is passed over and under the threads of the warp. As Hodges (1976, p. 188) explains, 'what dictates the type and size of fabric produced is not the orientation of the warp, but the means by which it is kept under tension'. The stories illustrate that materials are practically engaged, extending, focusing and refocusing business activities, and experientially bodily explored as business activities unfold. Already the stories in their emergence weave the social and the material together.

While there is simply no ending imposed on the activity of weaving, the gerund form is preferred (cf. Sandberg & Dall'Alba, 2009). From a here-and-now *weaving* reaches towards a past and a future, expressing intelligibility of being-in-the world as discourse broken up in spoken and written words presented in the form of stories. The stories that evolve do not require cohesive beginnings, middles and ends to be imposed. In between actualities and possibilities and with an account for what has been, five stories emerge as voices of the living, the not living and the voice of the researcher blend.

IN SUMMATION

Narrative is a form of language spoken by Aristotle's poet, an object of literature study, a tool for reality construction and a storification process as this chapter informs. In research concentrated on family, stories generally serve as method, medium and meaning. Grounded in a systems view, developmentalists direct attention to narratives in the form of personal life stories. Stories afford generativity, connecting family members across generations. As noted, developmentalists focus also on lexical and grammatical use of language in the narrative discourse in studies of children's production of narratives. Further, the chapter notes that family business and business history scholars show an interest in narratives, stories and storytelling. Family and business are presented as interacting systems that provide a context for storytelling.

The narrative approach, employed by Hamilton (2006) is highlighted. It draws on Ricoeur's (e.g. 1984) philosophical work on narrative and as emphasized, Ricoeur's notion of the pre-narrative has a certain affinity with Heidegger's (1962) notion of *Dasein*. By taking Roth's

(2018) conception of narrative into consideration, the chapter suggests a being-in-the-world narrative methodology, implied in which is a qualitative method that accentuates understanding, conceived of as the explicit form of interpretation.

The chapter also exhibits how empirical-oriented information has been generated and how stories unfold in between 'story partners' and are dealt with for contributing understanding of family business *as activities* and inspiring the development of a theory of socio-material weaving, conjoined with a narrative truth. The concluding chapter (Chapter 8) further discusses what theory development is about and what characterizes an alternative approach proposed in the form of a theory of socio-material weaving that aims at a narrative truth.

5. The Siljanstrand, the Siljansgården and the Green Hotel story

This chapter presents three stories in close relation to each other. The Siljanstrand and the Green Hotel story both centre on business activities of the first-generation Börjeson family, represented by Hans Erik Börjeson. Throughout 30 years, 1965–1995, Börjeson was the owner of Green Hotel, succeeded by his daughter Salka Börjeson Eynon. Since there is little information about members of the Börjeson family and the second-generation owner, the two stories are rather fragmentary and narrow in focus. I hope, though, that in spite of these limitations the chapter could give some insights into the sociality of activities interwoven with the material. It might also be of interest to observe that the transfer of the ownership of Green Hotel from the first to the second generation constructed an opportunity for the first generation to be involved anew in hotel business activities. Studies of succession in family business elicit that trans-generational transfer of ownership takes the family business from one stage to another and from one generation to another (e.g. Cadieux et al., 2002; Ibrahim et al., 2001). The transfer most often requires the predecessor(s) to disengage or retire from the business (e.g. Handler, 1994). As this chapter reveals, the former owner of Green Hotel did not disengage or retire but boomeranged back to a 'stage' of foundational character, yet, in relation to another business. In 2010, at the age of 83, Börjeson became the owner of Siljansgården, the name of which was changed to Siljanstrand.

On 30 June 2020, Siljanstrand was closed, however. During spring 2020, the coronavirus pandemic resulted in loss of guests and money. Hans Erik Börjeson died on 12 July 2020, and there was no opportunity for him to read the final version of this chapter and to consent to publish the quotes included. Therefore, parts have been deleted and the references made to Börjeson rely solely on text publicly available.

In close relation to the Siljanstrand story, the Siljansgården story evolves, re-actualizing a past that makes present activities associated with home building, guest home and education. It refers to the three-generation Alm family including Harald Alm, his children Signe and Bertil, and his grandchild Olof.

The three stories introduce 'owner' and 'manager' but indicate that these positions dissolve into activities that flow into other business-oriented activities. The Siljanstrand story involves two people whose relationship can be described as genuine, characterized by reciprocity, mutual dependence and trust (cf. Hall, 2003) as reflected by the expression 'we stick together like glue'. The Siljansgården story refers to familial relations sustained by blood and marriage, and to co-workers and children whose relationships cannot be detailed due to scarce information. Also mentioned are 'others', for example, builders and craftsmen with whom the storytellers interact.

THE SILJANSTRAND STORY

In 2010, Hans Erik Börjeson, then 83 years old, acquired Siljansgården, a number of buildings associated with guest home activities. The media informed that Börjeson did not believe he would become the owner. For both him and his daughter Salka, Siljansgården was something exceptional, situated on the shore of Lake Siljan as a precious glittering jewel. Salka got married at Siljansgården on 1 October 1988. Hans Erik Börjeson brought his daughter to the altar (Klockarås, 2010).

Siljansgården was converted into a hotel with the name Siljanstrand with about seven people involved in business-related activities. Owning Siljanstrand implied being immersed in a variety of activities. Börjeson lived at the hotel and interacted closely with Property Manager Mats Blomqvist. Sharing an office in the main hotel building, there were plenty of opportunities for ongoing face-to-face interaction. Börjeson and Blomqvist exchanged project ideas on a continuous basis and made plans for the careful renewal and development of the Siljanstrand buildings to attract guests and earn money. From 2014 to 2020 Mats Blomqvist was involved in renewal and development projects. He (personal communication, 10 July 2019) described the collaboration with the owner, to whom he referred as 'Hasse':

> We are working closely together ... we stick together like glue, I would say. We exchange ideas on various building projects, we share an understanding on what needs to be done and are committed to finding solutions on different matters ... Indeed, I would argue that most of the time we make decisions by consensus ... If I come up with an idea and make a suggestion for a project, Hasse usually responds in a positive way, saying: 'I trust you. What you

suggest is the right thing to do.' A most recent project concerns a house for which the drawing is already done and this winter it will be materialized in the form of a timber house. We are also in the process of moving two houses. Our imminent development project includes the renovation of a beautiful room for parties and festivities.

These activities reflect Börjeson's cultural achievement. Blomqvist (personal communication, 10 July 2019) pointed out:

Hasse has preserved the old materials and designs, being highly committed to doing so. Indisputably, he has made a cultural achievement. Unless Hasse had got his hands on Siljansgården it might have been converted to modern residential. That was the intention of one of the speculator, representing a real estate company that participated as bidder at auction on Siljansgården.

Materials have been used to help maintain the old construction of buildings with supporting beams and green roofs. The oldest building, from the 1300s, is one of the best preserved timber houses in Sweden. Moreover, old pebble walls and rose beds have been restored and new soil has been laid on the apple trees. Tällberg's oldest belfry has been moved to the courtyard. The shoreline has opened up and a bathing platform has been constructed (Siljanstrand Website, 2019).

When I met with Hans Erik Börjeson and Mats Blomqvist on 22 January 2020, I was informed that Siljanstrand consisted of 15 buildings and offered 20 rooms for hotel guests and facilities for 20 conference guests. Blomqvist (personal communication, 22 January 2020) emphasized:

Hasse has made a great cultural contribution, preserving the old buildings and I have been very fortunate to be a small part of that. His wish for the future is that one should continue to care for the buildings and their history. Siljanstrand is fantastic and working here invokes a wonderful feeling of contentment!

Blomqvist (personal communication, 22 January 2020) added: 'At present we are involved in a project regarding the construction of a house equipped with a kitchen that in the summer can be transformed into makeup rooms and lodges for actors. The idea is to allow the community theatre to give performances.'

Admittedly, for Hans Erik Börjeson, owning Siljanstrand meant being involved in business activities that were tightly intertwined with building and land materials. As Mats Blomqvist (personal communication, 22

January 2020) explained, they were always involved in construction projects and in that process they paid close attention to the view of Lake Siljan so as not to be obscured by houses that were enlarged or added. Siljanstrand is associated with culture, beauty and history (Siljanstrand Website, 2018). From the viewpoint of Börjeson, Siljanstrand was a place that inspired creative thinking as it encouraged the development of new ideas and visions of the future (Klockarås, 2010).

Circumstances changed. The spread of coronavirus strongly impacted the hotel and the number of guests staying at the hotel decreased. In spring 2020, the projects that aimed at offering more guests inspirational and joyful stays at Siljanstrand were cancelled. Mats Blomqvist left Siljanstrand on 30 June. Hans Erik Börjeson died on 12 July at the age of 93, and Siljanstrand was closed (Mats Blomqvist, personal communication, 26 November 2020; Siljanstrand Website, 2021).

Siljanstrand activities re-actualize a past, glimpses of which are provided next by the Siljansgården story.

THE SILJANSGÅRDEN STORY

After World War I, Siljansgården, first called Grangården, was closely connected with business activities focused on sports and recreation, education for children aged 7–15, courses for adults and guest home lodging. These activities were constituted of interactions and relationships that extended through a three-generation family that encompassed Harald Alm, his children Signe and Bertil, and the grandchild Olof.

Building a Home

In 1916, Signe Bergner went to Tällberg. The process of filing for a divorce from her first husband had started and she sought a place to build a home all of her own. Harald Alm (1969, p. 12) described what happened when she approached a crossroad in Tällberg: 'As she approached a crossroad she encountered a man. She inquired if there were some vacant land to buy. "Actually, there is", the man replied.' Signe acquired a piece of land grading off to the shoreline of Lake Siljan where there were grass fields, juniper and rose bushes and birch trees. Architects and craftsmen were hired and the forming of a home was initiated, mainly financed by Signe Bergner through selling old Chinese things in a boutique that was set up in Stockholm (Alm, 1969).

In Mrs Bergner's newly purchased land, as customary in Dalarna, a two-storey house was raised in the middle of the courtyard. Timber coming from an old mill, consisting of logs that had been carved, drawn and knotted, was used. A mill stone was placed in front of the house to function as a coffee table. A gable house extension made space for a kitchen and a dining room. A small storehouse, a *härbre*, was set up. More houses were added, moved from different places in Sweden. A home called Grangården was built (Alm, 1969).

Signe was born in 1881 and grew up as an adoptive child with the priest family Bergner in Jämtland, a northern province of Sweden. She had taken a gymnastics director exam and had, in addition, studied needlework and home economics, and social hygiene in London.[1] For many years she lived in China and was married twice, first to Gunnar Andersson, a professor of geology who worked with leading Chinese scientists and as advisor to the Chinese government, then to Carl Gimbel, a wealthy and high ranking official in the International Salt Union. In the marriage with Professor Andersson the daughter Lilian was born. When the mother moved to Sweden, Lilian stayed in China with her father (Alm, 1969).

Signe Bergner's third husband was Harald Alm, whom she met in Stockholm when returning from China. The love between Signe and Harald has been described as passionate and as an essential driving force for their business engagements (Alm, 1969; Liljas, 2016). Harald Alm, born in 1897 in Stockholm, was interested in pedagogy and alternative approaches to bringing up and educating children. He obtained a Bachelor of Arts degree at Uppsala University. Signe and Harald married in 1927 (Alm, 1969).

In Tällberg, the Alm couple continued to build and develop the home they now shared, using materials such as timber, stone, grass and Chinese fabrics. Stones were moved, fences were raised and lawns were prepared for leisure and sports activities. The walls of the main building were wall-papered with Chinese fabrics, door mirrors were provided with Chinese motifs and an image depicting the Chinese goddess of mercy, Kwan-Yin, was placed in the main building in a room that was called the Chinese room. The construction and decoration of the Tällberg home were inspired by work of Swedish and foreign artists and reflected Signe's life experiences in China. Harald Alm (1969, p. 20) described the activities of his wife: 'She brought together furniture and things as you bring friends together to harmonize well. Invisible links between things and things and

between things and people created an atmosphere of home comfort …
With the building of the home came planning and design of the terrain.'

Sports, Recreation and Education Activities

Grangården became a sports and recreation home for school children. In
China, Signe nurtured similar plans but they were never implemented. In
cooperation with a Swedish-American friend she planned to open a gymnastics institute in Shanghai for Chinese girls with bound feet. Before
getting married to Carl Gimbel, Signe made it clear that as a married
woman she should have the right to pursue her profession as a gymnastics
director. Signe had also studied physical therapy and the organization of
physical therapy institutes in the United States and was eager to realize
her plans regarding a gymnastics institute. However, her husband came
to prioritize his own professional career. Harald Alm (1969, p. 10)
commented that Signe would have been 'like a golden bird at cocktails
parties, dinner and balls in the peculiar life that Westerners involved in
diplomacy and in the business world lived in the East'.

The name of Grangården was changed to 'Siljansgården'. Siljansgården
activities expanded and the Alm couple worried about financing the
expansion. Bank loans were taken, even friends and relatives were asked
for loans and if they were willing to grant bail. But, none granted bail,
anticipating the couple would soon stumble. Besides, Siljansgården was
seen as a non-profit company. As Alm (1969, p. 226) pointed out: 'We
came across a peculiar attitude: "Were you not a non-profit company
… you should not talk about money anymore".' Neither municipal nor
state funds provided financial support but with the help of Signe's contacts with the Swedish crown prince, later King Gustav VI Adolf, and
advertisements in national newspapers, Siljansgården gained increased
attention and especially from private sources that were more inclined to
give financial help (Alm, 1969).

Siljansgården evolved into a practical summer school, a boarding
school for boys and girls aged 7–15 and soon a winter semester was
added. The first Swedish free school was established, during the 1930s
and the 1940s nationwide known under the name of the Siljan School.
The children usually came from wealthy upper-class homes where the
parents were living abroad (Liljas, 2016). The school also offered an
array of education courses for adults, covering topics such as psychology, sociology, religion, philosophy, breathing techniques and rhythm,
drawing and cultural history, with Richard Roth, Heinrich Hanselmann,

Alfred W. Adler, Charlotte Bühler, the Thurstone couple, Alice Tegnér, Knut Lundmark and Poul Bjerre, among others, lecturing. With the participation of Fritz Jöde, singing and music courses were arranged and the foundation for a nationwide sing-song movement was laid (Liljas, 2016). From 1943 lyric weeks were organized. Signe and Harald Alm served as principals for the Siljan School and engaged also in organization and administration activities and in teaching courses.

Inspired by the reform pedagogy movements in the United States and Germany, Siljan School education was permeated with the idea of body and soul integration, highlighted by the heraldic weapon of Dalarna to which were added the Latin words *Veritas, Caritas, Labor*, which stand for Truth, Care, Work. Hence, nurturing the whole child was essential, which required socializing the child with others in the home; the home was considered a superior environment for education with homeschooling and everyday work intertwined (Liljas, 2016). 'I had experienced my childhood and youth school as something of an inferno. It was clear to me that children should not be forced to attend school of the type I have experienced. I wished to create a new school', Harald Alm (1969, p. 37) put forward. The idea of integrating body and soul meant that intellectual work was combined with sports and games, housework, physical terrain and clearing work, and that boys and girls should participate in the activities on equal terms (Alm, 1969).

Siljansgården with the inclusion of the Siljan School was presented as a cultural centre where people moved between houses, cottages and *härbren* on a sloping terrain where terraces were built and lawns were bordered by beautiful stone walls and hedges were furnished with sofas made of tree trunks, and tables of materials that came from an old wheel mill. As Alm (1969) further recorded, there were winding paths and small stairs leading people from one discovery to another.

Sorrows and Challenges

Signe Bergner-Alm died on 15 October 1945. Harald Alm was severely burdened by sorrow, being alone he thought about the point of living, but eventually realized that it was important to show that he was worthy of the love of his wife by moving on, caring for and developing further what they had accomplished together (Alm, 1969). The urn with the ashes of his beloved wife was placed under the floor in the Chinese room, in the main building of Siljansgården (Ahlström Söderling, 2019). 'My grief became my work', highlighted Alm (1969, p. 148), and while he was regaining strength to go on and also cope with a strained financial situation, another unexpected blow came that made financial matters worse. He was contacted by Signe's first husband Gunnar Andersson, who on behalf of his and Signe's daughter Lilian requested the reserved share she was entitled to according to law, which corresponded to a quarter of the value of the Siljan School. However, the mother had financed the building of the Grangården home using her own money. Harald Alm (1969, p. 150) expressed a feeling of being attacked:

> I felt attacked ... The requested amount of money was impossible for me to pay and executive auction would be the only solution and as a result, the daughter and the father would destroy the life work of the mother. In any case, the daughter would inherit a wealthy father.

Fortunately, with a lawyer's assistance the demands were suppressed. Still, Alm was forced to pay SEK 200,000, at the time a considerable amount of money. Alm (1969, p. 152) did not know if he would be able to continue being involved in education-related business activities and conveyed what he currently felt in the words: 'In spring greenery I heard the ground crying.'

Berit Ejder became Harald Alm's second wife. The couple engaged in business activities associated with Siljan School education, which also implied the challenge of dealing with the National Board of Health. At the end of the 1940s, a letter arrived pointing out that children had been admitted to a school not inspected by the National Board of Health. Applications for government grants for course activities, submitted by Alm, were regularly rejected. Work inspectors arrived and examined the working conditions. Instead of salary the workers obtained free vivre. From the viewpoint of Alm (1969, pp. 240–1, emphasis in original) the workers were not *employees* but *co-workers for Life*:

> The leader should not regard the so-called worker as a means, a means for earning money. Nor should the worker regard the company and the entrepreneur merely as a means for making money. The entrepreneur should not measure what the workers contribute solely in terms of financial value with an intention to run the company just for profitable reasons ... but should replace the currently loathsome terms 'manager' and 'leader' with the term 'organizational worker' – ultimately, we must all be *co-workers for Life*.

Another battle with the National Board of Health concerned homeschooling. In the marriage between Berit Ejder and Harald Alm, two children were born; Signe in 1948 and Bertil in 1950. The father taught his children at home even though homeschooling was banned with criminal consequences for those practising it. Three policemen arrived in Tällberg to pick up Signe but her father had already arranged for the daughter to be brought to a family some 60 kilometres away. On the morning of the next day, Signe was returned safely home (Alm, 1969). This event received major headlines in both the Swedish and foreign press. After much struggle homeschooling was permitted, provided it was handled by well-reputed teachers (Alm, 1969).

A new tragedy struck. In 1951, the children's mother Berit died, aged 31 years old. Harald Alm (1969, p. 175) was faced with two options: 'The Siljan School or the children. But there was only one option available: the children.' The operations of the Siljan School ceased. For assistance in helping with household and childcare activities, Alm contacted Annedore Keil in Germany. She had previously spent time in Tällberg working at the Siljan School. Ms Keil returned to Tällberg and stayed there for almost 20 years. During these years she also engaged in building projects in cooperation with Harald Alm (1969, p. 177), who greatly appreciated her help: 'I see her diligent caring hands.' To exemplify, a small cottage called the Sun cottage was furnished, the guest house was decorated for socializing events, lectures and parties, and a two-storey timber house called the Poet was built (Alm, 1969).

In 1967, on his 70th birthday, Harald Alm (1969, p. 243) reflected on 50 years of Siljansgården activities: 'What we accomplished over the years, children and people of our time benefit from ... at the same time, we have created a poem for future generations to enjoy, a song about love on earth.' The voices of Signe Alm and her son Olof Alm Keys indicate how this poem is recited by the succeeding generations.

In the Voices of Signe and Olof

After the death of Harald Alm in 1976, Signe Alm became the sole owner of Siljansgården. Already in 1973, at the age of 25, she had assumed responsibility for Siljansgården guest home activities since Harald Alm suffered from Parkinson's disease, which led to difficulties with balance, walking and coordination, and he was not able to actively participate in matters concerning Siljansgården. As Signe (personal communication, 23 January 2020) explains: 'It might well have started much earlier ... not surprisingly it developed ... My father was worried about how things would unfold and did not feel particularly good about how things developed.'

Engaging in hospitality business activities was quite a challenging and demanding task. Signe (personal communication, 6 September 2018) describes: 'I was involved in everything. I was also kitchen manager and cook. I wanted food to be prepared in a special way, not as purely vegetarian but somewhat like that, and the food was much appreciated by the guests.' Signe's son Olof (personal communication, 8 February 2021) adds: 'My mother was involved in the preparation and cooking of all food that was served.'

Signe (personal communication, 6 September 2018) cared deeply for the guests, and was committed to creating an atmosphere of home comfort. She also provided guided tours, showing the Siljansgården buildings. In 'her excellent way of telling, she brought the history of the courtyard and the houses to life', Frykman (2010, p. 1) emphasized.

Upbringing and Marriage

Signe recalls the sorrows her two-year younger brother Bertil and she had to deal with and the challenges they faced when growing up. In 1951 they were confronted with the death of their mother. Signe was three years old and Bertil one year old. Annedore Keil arrived in Tällberg to help the widower Harald Alm take care of the children and do the housework. Signe (personal communication, 6 September 2018; 23 January 2020) relates:

> It was not easy to grow up as a child in such a context ... we had a German house keeper; she was diligent in her practical work but was not very able to express maternal affection. I have some knowledge about childcare models used in Germany and in other countries and I have also experienced practical application of various models. Both Bertil and I showed our respect to Annedore ... at the same time, we felt that something was missing in our relationship to her – a feeling of home comfort and motherly care. As siblings we were very close and cared strongly for each other. Our father wanted to give us a good upbringing ... but people have different understandings of what is good for a child.

As previously mentioned, Siljan School activities, the meaning of which was summarized by the Latin words of *Veritas*, *Caritas* and *Labor*, focused on body and soul integration. It was important to create a home environment to integrate education (with an emphasis on homeschooling) with practical work. Harald Alm taught his children at home and as already noted (in 'Sorrows and Challenges'), homeschooling was severely criticized by the National Board of Health and even the police got involved.

Homeschooling for Signe and Bertil was followed by studies in the Swedish town of Lund, located some 700 kilometres south of Tällberg. After completing their studies Signe and Bertil returned to Siljansgården where Signe engaged in a variety of business-oriented activities. Bertil was more reluctant to do so and returned to Lund for studies in physics and mathematics, earning a Master's degree.

In the years to come Signe was faced with several challenges as she had to cope with a marriage that failed, bringing up a child all on her own and caring for her brother who fell ill. Signe was married to Kenneth Keys, who came from England. In 1985, they had a son, Olof. The couple never discussed sharing the ownership of Siljansgården. As Signe (personal communication, 6 September 2018) indicates, marital tension developed and eventually resulted in divorce:

> My husband was an Englishman, he was not a co-owner ... eventually, he decided to leave us, which I think was right for the reason that we were so involved in everything, gardening and many other things ... My husband did not contribute much, he did not speak Swedish ... as an Englishman it was not easy for him and he did not realize how much work that actually was needed and that he could not enforce his authority over everything. Nevertheless, I had nobody else but Kenneth and when he decided to leave I was left alone ... If Bertil had not fallen ill everything had turned out differently ... the power of 'if'... Yet, with the help of people coming from villages nearby and other places I managed quite well in creating a homely ambience at Siljansgården.

Olof (personal communication, 8 February 2021) informs that during the summer, high season for holiday guests, there were about 15 people involved in Siljansgården activities. Signe hired and trained people, who often returned to Siljansgården summer after summer. During autumn and spring, the least busy season, fewer people engaged in guest home activities. Except for sports holidays and special weekends, there were not very many guests.

When growing up on Siljansgården, Olof (personal communication, 8 February 2021) helped out with various things:

> For example, I served food to the guests and took care of the guests to make their stay at the guest home and their mealtime enjoyable ... I also liked to cook. For me it is very important to notice flavours and textures of food

and making the mealtime feel like a pleasant experience. I find human–food interaction particularly interesting and have written an essay on that. From my viewpoint the meal constructs opportunities for positive experiences. It provides a meeting point for family and friends and for people who do not know each other, enabling interchanges of information and positive thoughts and development of creative ideas. Also a coffee break constructs an opportunity for people to interact and sharing their thoughts and ideas. A coffee break is much more than just having a cup of coffee.

Changing Circumstances

Circumstances changed and Siljansgården was sold by executive auction. In 2010, Hans Erik Börjeson became the new owner. Signe and her son experienced a difficult time when having to leave Siljansgården. As Olof (personal communication, 8 February 2021) tells:

> We went through a difficult process. I gave up on the idea on awaiting an opportunity to return to Siljansgården. My mother, on the other hand, kept the dream of returning alive for a long time. I began my studies in sociology at Uppsala University but did not complete the studies. Currently, I am employed by a company called *Hemglass* for selling ice cream. Ice cream also provides moments for joy and positive experiences.

A number of changes were made by Hans Erik Börjeson as the Siljansgården guest home was converted into a hotel called Siljanstrand. Today, Signe is retired and lives in Leksand, a neighbouring village of Tällberg. For Signe (personal communication, 6 September 2018; 23 January 2020) Siljansgården signifies a special atmosphere, associated with old buildings and a garden that no longer exists. Siljansgården refers to the three-generation Alm family with building and land materials witnessing family members' involvement in a variety of business activities, sorrows and challenges, and dreams that never appear to come true of a life where Signe continues to grow vegetables and flowers in a garden of a guest home situated by the shore of Lake Siljan.

THE GREEN HOTEL STORY

The renewal and development of Siljansgården and the change of the name to Siljanstrand were manifested, in 2010, in a way that reminded Hans Erik Börjeson of the time when he as a young guide in 1950 made his first trip to Paris. At the festive opening ceremony of Siljanstrand that took place on the Siljan shore there were a great many people present. As the icing on the cake, the original bus from Paris (a 1948 Volvo) drove up and the owner of Siljanstrand was given the opportunity to address the audience with the very same bus microphone he used 60 years earlier (Rönnblad, 2010). The old bus brought a past alive associated with a balcony in Paris.

On a Balcony in Paris

In Paris, Hans Erik Börjeson (1974, p. 1) got the idea of starting a travel agency business:

> I was standing on a shallow balcony up in a house on Rue de Trevise in the ninth district of Paris. The cars, which came from Rue La Fayette and were going to les Grande Boulevardes, had been stuck in a queue on the narrow street ... Over the roof chimneys, which seemed almost like flower pots turned upside down, looking north I glimpsed the vaulted dome of Sacré Coeure. In the middle of the city, in 'l'heure bleu', Seine floated with newly-sprouted chestnuts like a green veil over the gray water ... But I thought of neither the traffic, the city, nor of the twilight. I had an idea that I could not let go of. Before I turned my back on the street and entered my room, which still smelled cyanide after smoking against vermin, I had decided to start a travel agency business, personally and meticulously set up to give the travellers something far greater than other travel agencies, a business that also would make me prosper financially ... Until the small hours, I had chosen the name of the company. It would carry my initials: HEB.

With the HEB travel agency business, charter travel was established in Sweden, significantly impacting growth in the tourism industry. After 22 years (1950–72), the HEB agency was sold but already by 1965 Börjeson had acquired Green Hotel, aware that he would not be able to personally engage in hotel business activities until several years later. Börjeson (1974, pp. 98–9) explains:

> I intended to leave my travel business by 1972 ... My life should not stay focused on endless discussions with southern European hotel hosts. It would not consist of meal vouchers, tour guides, and charter ... I would not go on working at a pace that made a month pass by as fast as a day, a year as a week. I would live again. Not worrying about financial matters and the unexpected that could annihilate most things. Instead, I would grab the pen again, avail myself to other things, trying to build something that was mine. Something worth leaving behind. Something lasting. The hotel fit very well into that picture ... A kind of manifestation of my longing for beauty. A confession to our souls, the forests, the mountains, the valleys. To the dark old winter

nights. The stormy autumn. The bright summer nights. To the origin of me – my corner of the world.

Three Friends Visiting Tällberg

In 1953, Hans Erik Börjeson paid a visit to Green Hotel in Tällberg. Two friends, living in Stockholm, went to Dalarna. Hans Erik and his childhood best friend Lennart, who wished to go skiing in the 'mountains', drove up in Hans Erik's first car, a Volkswagen, to Insjön, a village situated close to Tällberg. At the guest house in Insjön they were acquainted with a young woman, Thessan. The three friends decided to visit Tällberg, and have a good lunch at one of the hotels. Börjeson (1974, pp. 97–8) relates:

> It was such a glorious winter day. Heavy snow on the trees. Not a cloud in the sky. We parked the car at the Granberg shop and walked up the steep hill at the crown of which I saw a timber building, the Green Hotel. I stopped, amazed. This was the most beautiful scenery that met my eyes. In a strange way, my thoughts went to San Michele on Capri, Axel Munthe's villa, situated on the rock ledge, the sculptured loggia, the view over the Gulf of Naples towards Vesuvius. The hotel building and the view of Lake Siljan with mountains in the distance reminded me of San Michele. We got to the hotel and there when standing by the buffet table, the 'smörgåsbord', I made the decision to buy the hotel.

Green Hotel was originally a private villa. In 1917, Hilda Andersson, private secretary of Professor Gösta Mittag-Leffler, who also built a villa in Tällberg, invested money earned from trading stocks in the construction of a large timbered house with a large garden where she and her fiancé Baron Bennet could enjoy a life together. The title 'baron' designates nobility and a social class that usually excludes those who are not of noble heritage. Ninnie Green (in Tällbergs Byalag, 2007, p. 145) reveals: 'At the time there were restrictions, not allowing a marriage between a noble and a non-noble person. Anyway, Ms Andersson wanted a private residence that offered a genteel way of life.' Ten years later Hilda Andersson was faced with financial problems and the villa was sold. Lilly Crafoord became the new owner. In 1947, the married couple Ninnie and Börje Green acquired the villa. They added a new building and a swimming pool, converting the villa into a 30-room hotel, which became known as the Flower Hotel (Green Hotel Website, 2019; Tällbergs Byalag, 2007).

The railroad was built at the beginning of the 1900s (Chapter 1). The so-called Dollar-train, departing from Stockholm with tourists destined to the midnight sun in Lappland made a first stop in Tällberg where buses took the passengers to the Flower Hotel. An interview in 1983 with Ninnie Green (Tällbergs Byalag, 2007, p. 145) informs us that Tällberg became an increasingly attractive tourist destination and many tourists visited the Flower Hotel:

> Everyone was delighted by the beautiful place of clean air and water. We were the first stop to the midnight sun and Lappland ... We liked flowers and we had greenhouses. I remember that we welcomed our guests by giving them a small flower bouquet to put in the buttonhole and when leaving they also received a bouquet for the buttonhole.

In 1965, Hans Erik Börjeson signed the contract that confirmed he was the new owner of the Green Hotel. Six years later he was able to spend more time in Tällberg, realizing the dream of his own San Michele.

Making a Dream Come True

In December 1971, the moment finally came for the new owner of Green Hotel to stay longer in Tällberg: 'I would live my dream near Lake Siljan. Stay in Tällberg more than ever before and immerse in work, trying to create my own San Michele' (Börjeson, 1974, p. 99). The hotel was enlarged to attract more guests and facilities were built for the comfort of the employees, mostly women, who came from different places in Sweden, Kiruna, Stockholm and Gothenburg. Not only locales worked at the hotel. Börjeson (1974, p. 138) expressively describes the enlargement work:

> The sound of the swinging axes echoes over the region, log is added to log as when our ancestors built for themselves and their descendants. A small store-house, 'härbre', is formed with nature and of nature for inhabitants and for those travelling the world. For people, their recovery, thoughts, creativity and community with others. A gift for those who, for nearly a quarter of a century, accompanied me around the world, and a legacy to those who are about to take over. Of faith in life – not just in our own moment on earth.

Redesigning the terrace, the so-called Green room, a new interior plan was opened up, and a swimming pool equipped with underwater sound system and a descendible glass roof to be installed as a dance floor over the swimming pool was constructed. Old houses located in other parts of

Dalarna were purchased and moved to the Green Hotel courtyard. Green Hotel is today the largest hotel in Tällberg with a hundred rooms available for 200 guests. The owner is Salka Börjeson Eynon (Green Hotel Website, 2019, 2020; Tällbergs Byalag, 2007).

Art was a major part of Börjeson's life. He was born in 1927 in Stockholm and grew up in a family where both parents were artists. Hans Erik and his wife Maria started to collect arts in the 1950s and spent many summers in Saint Jeannet in France with their friends Pablo Picasso and Marc Chagall. Over the years they acquired more than 200 works, mostly paintings but also graphics and sculptures. The collection, which was called 'Greenverket', included works by Anders Zorn, Carl Larsson, Ivar Arosenius, Carl Kylberg, Pablo Picasso and Marc Chagall, among others (Tapper, 2018). Greenverket, also the name of a room in the Green Hotel delegated to host the art works, was one of Sweden's most famous private collections of arts as Annette Granlund, arts specialist at Buskowskis in Stockholm, emphasized: 'The collection at Greenverket has provided me with aesthetic experiences beyond the ordinary and I am extremely grateful for the many and long conversations about art that took place during my stays at the Green Hotel' (in Tapper, 2018, p. 1).

The art collection was sold at auction at Buskowskis in Stockholm in June 2018: 'The highlight of the collection was "On the Beach St Ives Cornwall England", a watercolour masterpiece painted by Anders Zorn in 1888, exhibited at the prestigious Zorn exhibition at the Petit Palais in Paris' (Tapper, 2018). 'To me art is sacred', said Börjeson (Press Release, 2018, p. 1) and continued:

> Living with art and having the opportunity to share it, as we have had the opportunity to do through Greenverket in Tällberg has been a true joy and something that enriched my entire life. Through art I have made friends for life and I have always felt a very close connection to art. Now I hope the art works can give the same joy and inspiration to someone else, who can also secure its future and place in history.

In 2010, Börjeson acquired Siljansgården, intending to use the money earned from the auction in 2018 for continual renewal and building projects related to the Siljansgården buildings and land. Börjeson (in Tapper, 2018, p. 1) explained:

> My enthusiasm and love for Tällberg is unchanged after all these years, and art has been a way for me to give back. Siljanstrand is my latest contribution to Tällberg, and Siljansgården is truly culture-laden. The oldest building is

from 1332 … Siljansgården has a dramatic past and moreover, it is beautifully situated by Lake Siljan, which is almost crawling under the eaves, spreading a stunning beauty.

Before projects and activities associated with the Siljanstrand hotel (to which Siljansgården was converted) came to an end, Mats Blomqvist (personal communication, 10 July 2019), who lives in Leksand, also accentuated the beauty of Tällberg: 'It fills my heart with joy to come here – every day … working here evokes a feeling of happiness because it is so damn beautiful.'

A COMMENT

The Siljanstrand and the Green Hotel story concentrate interest to first-generation activities and to the acquisition of a glittering jewel and the realization of a San Michele dream, leaving financial aspects and rational calculations aside. The Siljansgården story refers to the development of a Tällberg land with grass fields, juniper and rose bushes and birch trees and presents a three-generation family. From a hermeneutic-phenomenological horizon (Heidegger, 1962) the individuals introduced in the stories are beings-in-the-world, intimately involved *with* the world *with* others *with* materials. These beings move in between present actualities and future possibilities, recalling a past that draws our interest to cultural achievement, holistic treatment of body and soul, 'co-worker for Life' and to Flower Hotel, Paris and HEB activities. The activities bring in materials that are mainly related to buildings and land, actualizing a focus on *existential space* and *bodily lived place* as the concluding chapter will highlight (Chapter 8).

NOTE

1. See Ahlström Söderling (2019) for a detailed description of the first 24 years of Signe Bergner's life.

6. The Klockargården story

The Klockargården story emerges through the layering of voices belonging to members of the Sandberg family related by blood and marriage. It refers to Astrid and August Sandberg, their five children Kerstin, Gudrun, Lars, Per and Margareta, and their grandchildren Anders and Lars, illustrating their entwinement with business activities oriented towards a bakery, handicraft, sheep farming, textile education, guest home and hotel lodging and further, to a residential project called Bergbacken. The story refers to a five-generation family as it also mentions that the father of August Sandberg engaged in business activities and that the great-grandchild Hilma excels in slalom. Many other people immersed in Klockargården activities, not presented by name are referred to as 'others', for example, women weaving, knitting and sewing and men helping with building construction and carpentry work.

For more than 30 years Per Sandberg, the second youngest child of Astrid and August, engaged in owning and managing activities in close interactions with his wife Inger and their two sons Anders and Lars. Per Sandberg introduces the story by taking us on a guided tour to the Klockargården houses, cottages and *härbren* dispersed within an area of approximately 60 acres. There are 37 buildings with 42 rooms and 80 beds provided for holiday and conference guests, and rooms designed for craft artists. Klockargården is sometimes described as a little village in the village of Tällberg. In the summer, the hotel courtyard is filled with artists who rent a room or a cottage for exhibiting and selling their works. There is also a bakery that offers the guests fresh flatbread and soup with local ingredients, and an old taxi and petrol station that bring a sense of nostalgia.

The story indicates that Klockargården is a company that is sold and bought but of central concern is a Klockargården that dissolves into activities, interwoven with materials that relate to buildings and land. The story pays specific regard to words uttered by members of the Sandberg family about activities throughout nine decades, from the 1930s to the 2020s.

BEGINNING WITH A GUIDED TOUR

The Klockargården story begins with a guided tour to buildings and rooms where we stop and look at paintings and tapestries that adorn the walls. The display of art works, their motifs and colours are accompanied by Per Sandberg's recitations of poems written by Swedish poets, Karl-Axel Karlfeldt and Gustaf Fröding among others. Paintings by Stina Sunesson (1925–1998), who in the 1960s moved to Tällberg, have a special meaning for Sandberg. Her very last painting indicates that death is close. It shows her cottage in Tällberg in front of which flowers of bright colours grow. Extending above the roof of the cottage the flowers symbolize that a life has been lived (Per Sandberg, personal communication, 7 October 2020).

In addition, Winter Carl Hansson's painting of stairs of ages in the life of a human couple is of particular interest to our guide. It is decorated by *kurbits*. The old floral painting practised by painters from Dalarna on walls, doors and furniture with extravagant imaginative flowers sometimes mixed with biblical motives has become known as kurbits. The word 'kurbits', derived from Latin *cucurbita*, means 'pumpkin' (Kurbits, 2021). Per Sandberg (personal communication, 1 August 2018) points to the 100-year life curve that extends from birth through maturity to death, commenting on the ascendant and descendant modes of ageing:

> Here is the newborn baby and here is death … from birth, the life curve rises to a peak at fifty and then, it slopes downward and you are heading for the grave. It is a pretty dramatic painting; young and flashy and then old, weak and crooked … so I thought about reversing that curve. When the children leave their parents, the parents are actually reaching the peak of their life; they get a pension and are free to start travelling. The 100-year curve, which after fifty years describes a downward movement, turns up instead. This is a more positive portrayal of the stairs of age.

During more than 30 years Per Sandberg was the owner of Klockargården. The ownership unfolds hotel business activities constituted of interactions with his wife Inger, their two sons Anders and Lars, and others. Through building materials and other materials the activities are extended. Per and Inger were both born in 1942. On their 50-year anniversary in 1992 Per presented the positive up-turning life curve (Per Sandberg, personal communication, 7 October 2020).

'Klockargården' is a name originally given to a little deserted cottage that Astrid and August Sandberg, the parents of Per, bought in 1936, and is also associated with activities in which they were involved when becoming Tällberg inhabitants.

ASTRID AND AUGUST AND THE DESERTED COTTAGE

Rättvik, Laknäs and Insjön are villages located in the vicinity of Tällberg, on the shores of Lake Siljan. Astrid Sandberg (1905–1975) came from Rättvik and August Sandberg (1908–1985) from Laknäs. Astrid was an evangelist, guitarist and singer, and August a baker at his father's bakery. In 1890, you could go by train to Insjön and from there continue by steamboat to Laknäs where August's father had opened a bakery combined with a café. He benefitted financially from the lively steamboat traffic in the summer and from the sleigh traffic in the winter on Lake Siljan. People went ashore to buy bread and have a cup of coffee. From 1890 to 1914 water brought people together. In 1914, the railway was extended to Tällberg. Adjusting to infrastructural changes, August's father asked his son and his youngest daughter Maja to open a bakery and café at the newly built railway station in Tällberg. From 1914 the use of boats and sleighs considerably diminished (Klockargården History, 2020; Per Sandberg, personal communication, 7 October 2020).

Astrid and August married in 1932 and for some years they shared a home with the parents of August in Laknäs. In 1936, the Sandberg couple bought a small cottage in Tällberg. It had been deserted for seven years. The price was SEK 2500, a sum of money August borrowed from his big sister. The cottage was beautifully located alongside the public road, a thoroughfare for pedestrians, cyclists and car drivers. Its location helped construct opportunities for marketing and selling handicraft products. Every day, people passed by the cottage. After renovation, a handicraft shop was opened. It was called 'Klockargården', a name inherited from the former owner, Klockar Anders Ersson. 'Klockar' is a title originally used in the Middle Ages. When the priest was called to a death bed, the Klockar walked with a small clock in his hand before the priest. Eventually, his duties were expanded, encompassing singing and reading in church and other church-related services. Moreover, Klockar served as a teacher at the village school (Ahlund, 1994). It is customary in Dalarna to use the name of a farm or a house in addition to a person's first name, mother and father. Thus, Astrid was given the name 'Klockar mother' and August 'Klockar father'. 'Klockar' was also added to 'Per' and to the names of his siblings and children (Klockargården History, 2020; Per Sandberg, personal communication, 1 August 2018).

The handicraft shop marketed leather products such as wallets and photo albums. As a young evangelist, Astrid went on tours in the south of Sweden. The evenings were scheduled for preaching, singing and playing the guitar. During the day she had time for the hobby of making leather products. The hobby combined with other types of handicraft works and extended into Klockargården business activities. Astrid hired women who were particularly skilled in weaving and sewing (Per Sandberg, personal communication, 7 October 2020).

Now the family consisted of three children: Kerstin,[1] born in 1933, Gudrun in 1935 and Lars in 1939. The little cottage became too narrow and a bigger house was built. Friends introduced Astrid and August to a Danish diplomat family, who lived in Stockholm and used to visit Tällberg during the summers. The break-out of World War II in 1939 made it necessary to prepare for evacuation of the Danish family. An agreement was reached with Astrid and August to allow the diplomat to rent the newly built house, yet the Sandberg family was allowed to stay in the house until a threatening war situation emerged that required the diplomat family to leave Stockholm. The contract that was signed stipulated that Astrid and August and the three children should be prepared, within a time frame of 14 days, to move out of their home and let the Danish family settle. As circumstances turned out, evacuation of the family from Stockholm to Tällberg was never needed (Per Sandberg, personal communication, 1 August 2018; 7 October 2020).

Incomes received from renting out the house were welcome for the growing Sandberg family. Per was born in 1942 and Margareta[2] in 1947. The enlarged family also meant that more people became involved in business activities that expanded in association with handicraft, house construction and sheep farming. Per (personal communication, 1 August 2018) summarizes: 'Five siblings helped out as the business grew, involving in different activities.'

HANDICRAFT, HOUSE CONSTRUCTION AND SHEEP FARMING ACTIVITIES

Fabrics were woven, cloths were embroidered and dresses were sewn, attracting an increasing stream of customers to Klockargården. A bakery with a café was added to the handicraft shop and a terrace looking on to Lake Siljan was built. Among people visiting Astrid Sandberg's shop, a pharmacist named Gustaf Bernström and a builder by the name of Anders Diös expressed their admiration for her diligence and work. Margareta (personal communication, 7 October 2020), recalls: 'Anders Diös visited Tällberg quite often, asking his private chauffeur to make a stop at mother's café.' The two gentlemen identified a market for handicraft products outside of Tällberg, suggesting the establishment of Klockargården handicraft stores in two major cities of Sweden, Gothenburg and Västerås. Per Sandberg (personal communication, 1 August 2018) relates:

> Pharmacist Bernström from Gothenburg visited Tällberg … he saw mother's nice little shop, thinking that such a shop would fit well in Gothenburg. Pointing that out to her, he made her feel very proud and he asked if she would consider moving to Gothenburg. 'I have five children and it is not possible for me to move', mother replied. After a few years Bernström returned to Tällberg to let my mother know that he was not given up on the idea of establishing a handicraft store in Gothenburg and informed her that there was a vacant premise to rent. 'Our limited resources make renting and furnishing impossible, we do not have enough money', emphasized mother. 'But that does not matter. I am Chairman of a bank, Götabanken, so I am able to help with your financing', stressed Bernström. Right then, mother made up her mind to go to Gothenburg.
>
> When mother arrived in Gothenburg, Bernström arranged for a limousine to take her around the city. In 1951, she opened a handicraft store on Korsgatan 3, which was opposite to Ahlström's café. Mother hired an assistant, a textile teacher, to whom she assigned the task of taking care of the newly established shop. At first, the assistant was a bit hesitant about going to Gothenburg but eventually, made up her mind to go. She remained in the position as store manager for 28 years.
>
> And then there was another adventure … The builder Anders Diös too made a suggestion for market expansion: 'I am in the process of building business premises in Västerås. You are a creative and diligent person and there is opportunity for you to establish a store in Västerås.' Now, mother did not dare to invest and rent a premise.

The Klockargården handicraft works attracted an increasing stream of customers, including customers of royal descent. In the late 1940s the Swedish princess Sibylla and two of her children, the princess Christina and the crown prince Carl Gustaf, paid a visit to Klockargården (Tällbergs Byalag, 2007). Between the years 1946 and 1985 ten handicraft stores were run at different places in Sweden. Textile workers manufactured table cloths, shawls, blankets, furniture fabrics and carpets. As many as a hundred talented women engaged in weaving, knitting and sewing. The women worked in their homes. 'Klockargården' was equated with quality and became known by people around the world (Klockargården History, 2020).

Handicraft activities were also extended through building materials. An old building bought at auction in Dalarna was refurbished and a store was added to make room for handicraft works. An old timber frame was brought to Klockargården to be used for construction of a textile studio. Old timber houses located in other places of Dalarna were identified and purchased by Astrid Sandberg. The houses were dismantled and transported to Klockargården where her husband with the help of local builders and carpenters reassembled the houses, integrating them with existing buildings (Klockargården, 2020; Per Sandberg, personal communication, 1 August 2018).

August Sandberg left the baking profession to engage in house building activities. Within the following two decades he brought home numerous houses. His son (Per Sandberg, personal communication, 1 August 2018) informs:

> Before dismantling a house and bringing it to Klockargården, my mother and father went to see it, under careful examination making sure it was a good house ... Father coordinated everything and was responsible for the practical work. After all, my father was the practitioner and my mother the idea maker. Mother snapped up objects that suited well the existing Klockargården buildings. She used to sit at the kitchen table sketching and planning ... We were keen on using solid timber logs. All Klockargården buildings are made of old timber logs.

Handicraft activities were combined with sheep farming. In connection with these activities, Per Sandberg (personal communication, 1 August 2018) emphasizes tradition and nature:

> We cannot imagine buying a new house or cottage but an old house and cottage with tradition ... it must be made of timber and nothing else but solid timber ... This implies proximity to nature which is also reflected by sheep farming activities with which we engaged for a period of time. The growing grass around Klockargården obscured the view of Lake Siljan ... We had 250 sheep grazing lawns and slopes, allowing for a view of Lake Siljan to be enjoyed. And, by using sheep wool we were able to weave very fine textiles. Our family perspective involves humans and animals – a wholeness that brings nature and business together ... However, we were faced with fierce competition from sheep farmers in Australia; wool came into the Swedish market at a lower price and we were forced to bring sheep farming to an end. At least we had been able to take care of the view in the village for a period of time.

TEXTILE EDUCATION ACTIVITIES

Handicrafts associated with weaving gained enhanced focus through business-oriented education activities, in 1959 presented as the School of Textiles, a boarding school that invited young women who wished to become textile teachers to apply to the courses that were offered with a church profile. After completing a textile education in Stockholm, Gudrun Sandberg became involved in teaching courses at the School of Textiles as her sister Margareta (personal communication, 7 October 2020) informs. A young woman by the name of Inger, a student admitted for textile studies, participated in the very first textile course. Six years later, in 1965, she married Per Sandberg.

Weaving courses at the School of Textiles at Klockargården in Tällberg were not the only alternative available for Inger as she also took under consideration textile courses offered at Säterglättan, an institute of crafts located in Insjön. Inger Sandberg (personal communication, 7 September 2018) recalls the choice she made in the 1950s and what it was like to arrive in Tällberg:

> Tällberg is fantastic! I came from Grängesberg, an industrial community in Dalarna ... To come here and experience the beauty of Tällberg ... I never forget how it felt to arrive in Tällberg and be a student at the School of Textiles. Klockargården was not an obvious choice for me, however. Textile courses were also offered by Säterglättan in Insjön ... I gathered information about the courses, also asking my father for advice. Finally, I made up my mind to apply to the School of Textiles at Klockargården ... It is a bit strange, though, how things turn out in life ... it could as well have been Insjön.

Per Sandberg (personal communication, 1 August 2018) recalls the arrival of Inger at Klockargården and what he felt when he first laid eyes on her: 'She came here in 1959 to pursue an education for textile teachers ... I was seventeen and she was also seventeen and we were immediately attracted to each other.' Inger (personal communication, 7 September 2018), addressing Per as 'Pelle', adds:

> I was seventeen when I met Pelle, now I am turning seventy-six ... My intention was to become a textile teacher so, in addition to the Klockargården textile courses, I participated in courses in Stockholm at 'Libraria' and in Gothenburg at 'Tillskärarakademin'. Then, I returned to Tällberg and continued with textile work at Klockargården ... My mother-in-law wanted me to start working with church textiles and so I did. To give an example, I sew three vestments, liturgical garments, to be worn by priests.

By participating in textile courses at Libraria, an atelier in Stockholm that developed into a company producing church textiles (Lindqvist, 2020), and at Tillskärarakademin, a school in Gothenburg that offered courses in textile handicraft professions, Inger was qualified for work as a textile teacher.

Astrid Sandberg had been encouraged to start an education focused on textiles, confidently assured that the Swedish government would provide financial support. The School of Textiles activities were arranged in the form of annual courses but at the beginning of the 1960s, due to changing financial circumstances, education activities were organized as short courses. The idea of being involved in guest home activities in parallel to education activities was brought up. Per Sandberg (personal communication, 1 August 2018) tells:

> With financial support provided by the Swedish government my mother started the School of Textiles. The government grants were supposed to cover costs for teachers' salaries. The first courses were offered in 1959. However, the premises of the government changed. Private schools were no longer granted financial support ... Lacking that kind of resources we were forced to organize all teaching under our own regime. During 1959 and 1960 annual courses were given but those courses had to be closed down quite abruptly. So we arranged for short courses instead and the idea of offering hotel-like lodging came up. Student rooms could be used as guest rooms when students were not attending courses. In parallel to textile education, guest home was run.

INVOLVED IN HOTEL BUSINESS ACTIVITIES

The number of tourists in Tällberg steadily increased and in the 1960s the focus shifted away from education and guest home activities to hotel business activities. Klockargården buildings were renovated and enlarged. In the late 1950s, a timbered mansion was built that now serves as the main hotel building. The mansion was constructed out of old houses that were moved from other places in Dalarna to Klockargården. The so-called Tänger house, with a threshing floor where farmers had thrashed grains for centuries, provides room for weddings and conferences. An old mill, brought from the shore of the Dal River, was integrated with the main building, and a large barn was divided to be used as wings. In interactions with his wife Astrid, local builders and carpenters, August Sandberg coordinated the renovation and enlargement work, ensuring careful integration of the new buildings with the existing buildings (Klockargården History, 2020, Klockargården Website, 2018).

Stables, lofts and barns were also set up to construct opportunities for artists to exhibit and sell their works. One of the artists resides in a house with an open fireplace with a stone wall consisting of iron ore, cupper, porphyry and a piece of a stone originating in outer space, a meteorite that hit earth 377 million years ago and formed a crater where Lake Siljan is located (Chapter 1). A table put on the wall behind the fireplace provides information about the stones. The house is called 'Fejset' since it was used as a cowshed where a person kept the fire burning and maintained fire watch throughout nights to keep the cows warm. From Per Sandberg's viewpoint it is essential to use materials that belong to Dalarna, caring for history and traditions. Residents recognize porphyry as a defining symbol of the province of Dalarna (Per Sandberg, personal communication, 1 August 2018; 7 October 2020).

Five Siblings: Five Owners and Managers?

Five siblings, representing the third generation of the Sandberg family, Kerstin, Gudrun, Lars, Per and Margareta, residing in Tällberg, were involved in a variety of Klockargården hotel business activities. Expansion of activities in the 1960s put demands on setting clear roles and responsibilities so everyone knew what was expected in terms of tasks and duties. As there was no room for five managers and five owners, a tough decision had to be taken regarding Klockargården ownership and management, and it was Astrid Sandberg who made that decision. Per Sandberg (personal commutation, 1 August 2018), reveals:

> It was mother's dilemma ... she realized that Klockargården hotel activities expanded and that there were different views and meanings expressed among the five of us. She contacted a family lawyer for advice. He emphasized: 'Even if it is difficult, you have to make a decision with the future of Klockargården in sight. You must appoint *one* responsible person.' We had a family meeting ... I experienced the meeting to be rather dramatic ... Mother announced that she had decided that Pelle takes over ownership and responsibility for the Klockargården hotel business. At the same time she ensured my sisters and my brother to be well compensated. So it was a fair decision and a fair division.

Per, who studied business administration and participated in several management courses, concentrated on owning and managing activities.

Kerstin engaged in administrative activities which included recording and analysing financial transactions, Gudrun in activities associated with the handcraft shop and the café, and Lars in activities related to the Klockargården land and forest (Per Sandberg, personal communication, 1 August 2018; 7 October 2020). Margareta (personal communication, 7 October 2020) pursued an education for 'Ekonomiföreståndare' and assumed the position as Head of the household, which implied hiring and training kitchen staff, overseeing and working alongside the staff.

Eventually, Margareta (personal communication, 7 October 2020) moved to another place in Dalarna:

> I have planned to continue working as 'Ekonomiföreståndare'. However, there was limited time for taking care of my little children. I could not finish my work on time. There were always things to do after hours. My husband ran his own business. I coped for some years, finally realizing that a change was needed, so I left Klockargården and Tällberg.

Kerstin and Per still live in Tällberg. Their brother Lars died in 2014 and their sister Gudrun in 2019. Kerstin (personal communication, 7 October 2020) emphasizes: 'I was born in Tällberg and I grew up here, I have lived my whole life in Tällberg. It is my home. That encompasses everything.'

Inger Sandberg (personal communication, 7 September 2018), the wife of Per, became increasingly involved in Klockargården activities: 'I have sewn all curtains and decorated all rooms … I have made everything, always making sure that everything is beautifully arranged everywhere.' 'Inger was hostess, designer and decorator', summarizes her husband (personal communication, 1 August 2018).

Hotel Klockargården guests are allowed to bring their pets, a dog or a cat. Inger designed and decorated a four-poster bed including a basket for a dog with liver candy on the pillow and soft dogs to play and cuddle with. Inger and Per's own terrier, Polly, usually resided in the reception area for welcoming the guests. Yet, an open attitude to bringing pets to the hotel must be balanced with the risk of triggering allergic reactions in people. Inger Sandberg (in Hällberg, 2006, pp. 1–2) commented:

> We have always had an open attitude to animals at the hotel but now we have taken it a step further. Animals are family members! Why should the dog be forced to stay at home and why should pet owners have less comfortable and nice rooms? … We never experienced any problems during the years Polly was here. Polly loved to be here and reluctantly left the hotel in the evening

... Conference guests even expressed some feelings of disappointment when Polly was not showing up on time in the morning.

Struck by a Huge Tragedy

Inger and Per Sandberg had two sons: Anders, born in 1968, and Lars in 1971. Per's intention was to let his youngest son assume full responsibility for the Klockargården business activities. Lars was expected to succeed his father as owner and CEO, but these expectations were never realized. A huge tragedy struck the family. Lars died at the age of 28. Per Sandberg (personal communication, 1 August 2018) tells:

> Lars was trained as hotel manager, experienced from running other hotels in Sweden. However, his career was abruptly interrupted. Having stomach pains, he went to the hospital. I have diabetes and as there are forms of diabetes that are directly inherited, Lars was tested for diabetes. He was put on a restricted fasting diet but his health condition deteriorated rapidly. It appeared that Lars suffered from Addison's disease. Diagnosed too late there was no treatment. Lars should have been given nutrition. The doctor wrongly put him on a fasting diet. Within three or four days he died ... This happened in 1999 ... faced with this huge tragedy we could hardly breathe ... Big brother Anders, who held a position as manager in Sälen and worked as international ski instructor, returned to Klockargården and assumed the position as CEO ... We were going through a most difficult time but we gradually managed. Anders stayed at Klockargården for 18 years.

By the end of the 1960s, a ski lift was inaugurated in Tällberg. As Anders Sandberg (personal communication, 7 October 2020) tells, his father engaged in various matters in the village of Tällberg, among other things he saw to it that a ski lift was built. Anders excelled in slalom and became an international ski instructor in Sälen.[3] In the 1990s, he was head of 150 ski instructors. He also tells that during summer breaks he went home to Tällberg, engaging in Klockargården hotel activities. In 1998, he met Susanna, his wife to be, who worked at Klockargården. Susanna and Anders lived in Sälen for a couple of years.

When Lars died, Anders terminated the engagement with ski instructor management in Sälen. In spring 2000, Susanna and Anders returned to Klockargården where Susanna assumed the position of Hotel Manager but she was not very keen on using this title, according to her husband (personal communication, 7 October 2020). Her main focus was reception, bookings and arrangements of conferences, activities for which she brought her experiences from earlier involvement in travel agency activities and from using sophisticated computer systems. Anders assumed the position of CEO, involved in activities with a strong focus on marketing. He (personal communication, 7 October 2020) reveals: 'Pretty soon I realized the need for increased market orientation and as a result, turnover went up and we began to earn more money ... maybe we were lucky too ... my father had made extensive preparations for launching new services that included weekend packages, for example.'

From the perspective of Per Sandberg (personal communication, 1 August 2018; 7 October 2020) it is important to preserve the Dala atmosphere, which is associated with the Klockargården and the Tällberg traditions. Old buildings and furniture, paintings decorated with kurbits and tapestries made by Stina Sunesson, the Tällberg local costume, and traditions such as 'Lissjul' and midsummer contribute to the so-called Dala atmosphere. Lissjul is celebrated on the Saturday before Second Advent with people invited to a walk lighted by marshals through the Tällberg village. Guides wearing folk costumes take care of the visitors at the Klockargården Christmas market. In June, the maypole is raised, around which dancing and singing take place to celebrate midsummer (Klockargården, 2020; Tällbergs Byalag, 2007). As Graburn (2001, p. 6) submits: 'Tradition was the name given to those cultural features which, in situations of change, were to be continued to be handed on, thought about, preserved and not lost.'

From the perspective of Anders Sandberg (personal communication, 7 October 2020) it is important to reflect on 'travel reason'. There are eight hotels in Tällberg and why is Klockargården worth paying a visit to? In response to that question there was enhanced focus on activities oriented towards entertainment, and the Salon of Culture ('Kultursalongen') was established. Father and son saw it as important to develop services that were unique in comparison with services offered by the other hotels in Tällberg. Ideas proposed by Per Sandberg were materialized by his son, who used a more modern format for the Klockargårdens offerings and identified channels for digital marketing. Per Sandberg (personal communication, 7 October 2020) explains:

Anders extended the traditional cultural elements to include modern elements. For a compromise I suggested a three-act: The first act was directed by me with a focus on the traditional as manifested in the folk costume, and the second act by Anders with a focus on 'Broadway'. During the third act we met on the dance floor, the symbolic middle, where the traditional and the modern mixed. This is very much the idea behind the establishment of the Salon of

> Culture … showing up in folk costume with tassels attached to your knees on the trousers is simply not enough to attract hotel guests.

Merely the word 'Salon of Culture' gained interest. An inauguration ceremony was held in the presence of the Governor of Dalarna which sparked further interest for the new format of entertainment launched by Per and Anders Sandberg. The Salon of Culture allows for an audience of 350 persons to enjoy shows, concerts, theatres and dancing. There were also special summer offerings as Anders (personal communication, 7 October 2020) informs:

> In the summers we also held barbeque evenings and invited troubadours to entertain our guests. But things had not turned out the way they did without the help of my father, we complement each other. Even if you disagree on certain matters and involve in tough fights, the positive side outweighs the negative side.

Anders and his brother Lars discussed how to develop the summer offerings. They also shared a dream of building a hotel chain, owning and managing hotels located in different geographical areas. However, their ideas and dream were never realized. Anders (personal communication, 7 October 2020) tells:

> The summer activities were taking place before Lars died, and Lars and I discussed ways to develop further the activities. Lars was also an entrepreneur. I recall our conversation the last summer he lived … we went for a boat trip on Lake Siljan … Lars then worked at a chain hotel in Falun.[4] He emphasized: 'Together we shall build and run hotels as part of a chain.' When he died, the sorrow was incredible … we never got the chance to realize our dream. My brother was fantastic at lobbying and networking and I am confident he would have acquired several hotels outside of Tällberg just through his way to interact with and relate to people. As opposed to him I easily end up discussing details. It had been most exciting to see what we had been able to accomplish together … this, we talked about during our last boat trip ... in the autumn he went away … I think his death made me make up my mind to return to Tällberg.

After 18 Years

In 2004, Susanna and Anders had a daughter, Hilma. Anders (personal communication, 7 October 2020) recalls: 'When she turned four, I realized that she had a great talent for skiing and I taught her how to make slalom ski turns. The whole family is passionate about slalom.' Hilma excelled in slalom and Anders regarded it as a more important task to engage in his daughter's training and told his parents that he wished to be separated from his current position and work. Eighteen years had passed. His father (personal communication, 1 August 2018) points out:

> Anders stayed at Klockargården for 18 years ... his daughter competes in slalom and because Anders is an international ski instructor he is now training his daughter. When the daughter began at primary school the family moved to Mora[5] where she became a member of the ski club, given the opportunity to invest more in slalom with her dad as coach ... Anders explained to me that he had done his years at Klockargården and that he now wished to leave ... Very gently he informed me about his change of heart ... The change in ownership and management now meant that we had to find a person willing to take main responsibility and at the same time, ensuring the preservation of the traditions and the Dala atmosphere associated with Klockargården.

According to Per Sandberg (personal communication, 1 August 2018) it was not important to scan the hotel market for potential buyers to get the highest possible price:

> How can we make sure that Klockargården traditions and atmosphere will be preserved? Whom can we trust? Inger and I are not prepared to start again at an age of 75–76 years, shouldering the overall responsibility. So we hand-picked a good man, Staffan Malmqvist, who already was involved in hotel businesses in Tällberg.

Anders Sandberg (in Ingels, 2017, p. 2) submits:

> We were contacted by many persons interested in running the hotel. My previous contacts and collaboration with Staffan ascertained me that he shared my view of the market, sales and operations of hotels in Tällberg. It takes time to get everything together, many aspects of a hotel business must be taken into considerations and it took a year before we reached an agreement. Staffan takes over Klockargården ... It is fantastic to be able to preserve the Klockargården traditions in combination with a refined way of looking at competition. It is important to reach out into the world and identify market niches ... On these matters, Staffan and I are like-minded. Klockargården will continue to be a strong brand when we take the next step in business development.

Per Sandberg (personal communication, 1 August, 2018) admits:

> We have put so much of ourselves and our emotions into our doings ... we have felt strongly about maintaining a high level in quality in handicrafts,

house construction and furnishing … We never separated family from business. We never contacted an architect or a consultant for learning how to build and run a business … it has been a process … Now, we are taking a step in a new era but in a way that accords well with our idea of preserving the traditional.

In 2018, Staffan Malmqvist acquired 60 per cent of the Klockargården shares from Anders Sandberg, who since 2002 was the owner of 60 per cent of the Klockargården shares. Per Sandberg (personal communication, 1 August 2018) comments:

> I had already transferred the majority of shares to Anders. When Lars died I was forced to reconsider the transfer of ownership and management … Anders got 60 percent and I kept 40 percent, and for technical reasons, tax reasons and all sorts of reasons we decided to finalize a deal with Staffan, letting him buy 60 percent at one single occasion instead of doing it in stages … we had no heir.

After 18 years of involvement in Klockargården owning and managing activities, Anders Sandberg left the position as CEO but his wife Susanna continued working at Klockargården for two more years. The new majority owner was very impressed by the work of Susanna, her diligence and knowledge and the good way in which she structured work regarding reception, bookings and conferences, and asked her to stay on for two more years (Anders Sandberg, personal communication, 7 October 2020). Also Per Sandberg, co-owner with 40 per cent of the shares, continued to be involved in Klockargården activities, primarily with a focus on cultural events and guiding tours (Carlsson, 2018).

In 2019, Staffan Malmqvist attained full ownership of Klockargården. From the perspective of the new owner (personal communication, 9 October 2020) the Klockargården traditions originate in the history of handicraft works, the School of Textiles and the chain of handicrafts stores. This is the fundament, according to him. As owner and CEO of Klockargården, Malmqvist regards it as essential to keep reminding himself and others of the Klockargården history and traditions:

> The other night I introduced a show in the Salon of Culture, telling the audience about the history of Klockargården. I mentioned that the former owner, Klockar Per, helped to construct this house, which is made of timber logs. He went through mires to harvest moss to be used for filling gaps between the logs. This, I told in a trembling voice … I have a very strong feeling and a great respect for what was done in the past.

Owning and managing activities describe a lifestyle; a way to be that includes caring for history and traditions, making them alive in the present with a future in sight. The activities are interwoven with building and land materials that witness the predecessors' walks and works. Staffan Malmqvist (personal communication, 9 October 2020) explains:

> The materials have something to tell you and we do not always need to look for new things and lay new trails. It is important to care about trails laid out in a past. When I am asked to define the so-called selling point of Klockargården, I refer to feelings, quietness, the genuineness emanating from history and traditions and to the beauty of Tällberg.

Per Sandberg (personal communication, 4 April 2020) summarizes:

> First Anders sold his 60 percent and then I sold my 40 percent. Klockargården is now part of a hotel group owned by Staffan Malmqvist. It includes Gyllene Hornet in Tällberg, and Masesgården, a health resort located in Leksand. The hotel 'Villa Långbers' in Tällberg is leased by Staffan, the primary reason being the achievement of synergies through collaboration across tourist programmes, bookings and allocation of staff. Due to the corona virus outbreak the hotels lost most of their guests, however. This was a new and unexpected development that caused severe financial problems. For me personally it was financially advantageous to get involved in another project, the Bergbacken project.

The former principal owner of Klockargården became involved in a residential project called 'Bergbacken' with the intention of 'creating accommodations that blend in with the surrounding environment of Tällberg with a concern for nature and culture' (Måg, 2012, p. 1).

INVOLVED IN THE BERGBACKEN PROJECT

The Bergbacken project concerns activities such as marketing, preparing contracts and constructing houses within an area that comprises approximately 60 acres, located in southern Tällberg overlooking Lake Siljan. There are also plans for condominiums in an adjoining area called 'Kusbacken' (Måg, 2012).

As Per Sandberg (in Måg, 2012, pp. 2–3) points out, there is reason for proceeding slowly through the project:

> It may very well take 15 years or longer to implement the project. It is of crucial importance that the work is done with greatest care. We have already been granted building permits ... There needs to be living areas of approxi-

mately 3000 square metres with enclosed courtyards open to the lake. Roof slopes, house designs and other aspects of house construction in Tällberg must comply with certain regulatory requirements stated in a building program. There are green areas that have a construction ban and there is prohibition for future cutting ... I am also about to put up a smaller house for provision of information about the project. Over the years I have been involved in several building projects and the ordinal number of the house under construction amounts to fifty.

In spring 2020, Per Sandberg (personal communication, 4 April 2020) was encumbered with great sorrow over the loss of his wife Inger: 'Inger died on 27 March from pancreatic cancer. She underwent surgery and chemotherapy treatment for a year to get rid of the cancer. To be in so much pain, death actually seemed like a relief. I and Anders were by her side.' Because of the risk of corona infection only the immediate family was present at the funeral. The services took place in the church of Leksand where three vestments, liturgical garments, sewn by Inger, were exhibited. The cloth that covered the coffin was also designed and sewn by Inger. The funeral ceremony was filmed, leaving father and son moments to remember on the day of the inurnment ceremony.

A few months later Per Sandberg underwent a surgical amputation of his right leg above the knee. His son Anders (personal communication, 7 October 2020) conveys:

> Sometimes I think ... I do not know if I have been able to process the death of my mother ... Things have also happened to my father ... we have nevertheless been keeping busy, involving in the Bergbacken project and maybe it is a way to keep sorrow at a distance ... As for the Bergbacken project the corona pandemic seems to have had a great impact on people's willingness to buy lots and build apartments. Because of corona, demands for lots and apartments have risen. There is so much to do that I have decided to quit my job in Mora. I like very much being involved in the Bergbacken project, it is so much fun.

Bergbacken is also the name of a big house that was purchased at the beginning of the 1960s. Despite having not given the highest bid at auction for the house, the Sandberg family, known for careful preservation and maintenance of Tällberg buildings, was chosen. For some years Bergbacken served as an annex to Klockargården to make more rooms available for students at the School of Textiles and for an increasing number of holiday guests (Per Sandberg, personal communication, 7 October 2020).

Many years ago, Inger and Per Sandbeg were the residents of Bergbacken. In this very house their first-born son Anders took his first steps when holding onto the edge of the kitchen table. Today, Per and Anders again are working alongside each other – in Tällberg, which Anders (personal communication, 7 October 2020) associates with 'home': 'Tällberg is a place that allows for a view of Lake Siljan that takes my breath away every day. It is a place where you feel at home … Tällberg is "coming home".'

A COMMENT

The Klockargården story indicates that there is always something going on. For example, Per Sandberg is currently involved in a project numbering 50 in a countable series of projects. Members of the Sandberg family can be presented as 'wayfarers', to use a concept introduced by Ingold (2011). As beings-in-the-world they are *moves*, threading their ways in entwinement with business activities in, through, between and around houses, cottages and *härbren*. This implicates buildings as 'knots'. A knot is a house where the lifelines of, or the paths made by the wayfarers meet, although not contained within the house (Ingold, 2011).

We recognize activities along new lines in association with owning activities with which Staffan Malmqvist is entwined, and in association with lines threaded by the predecessors Astrid and August Sandberg. In such a meshwork of lifelines (Ingold, 2011) there is no single path along which a history of business activities unfolds and accordingly, there is no single story plot to present. Klockargården dissolves into a variety of business activities that extend and reorient through building and land materials in connection with which *existential space* and *bodily lived place* become a focus of interest (see Chapter 8).

NOTES

1. Today, her family name is Sanfridson.
2. Today, her family name is Aspman.
3. Sälen is a ski resort in Dalarna.
4. Falun is situated about 54 kilometres north of Tällberg in Dalarna.
5. Mora is a municipality in the vicinity of Tällberg.

7. The Åkerblads-Tällbergsgården story

The Åkerblads-Tällbergsgården story introduces Tällbergsgården hotel business activities in close relation to and as an extension of Åkerblads hotel business activities. Christina Åkerblad, her sons Anders and Jerk and their families tell about their present future-oriented entwinement with these activities and the ways in which they relate to and use materials associated with building and land. The Åkerblads buildings provide 73 rooms for hotel and conference guests, and the Tällbergsgården buildings make 33 rooms available for hotel and conference guests. Anders is the owner and CEO of Åkerblads, and Jerk the owner and CEO of Tällbergsgården. Jerk shares the ownership of Tällbergsgården with his wife Carina. 'Ownership' and 'owner' unfold activities that are crossed by and convergent with other business-oriented activities.

In association with Åkerblads we listen to the words of Anders and his wife Gunilla, their daughters Rosanna and Lovisa and their son-in-law Elias Granat Åkerblad (Rosanna's husband) and to Fredrik Svedberg, whom Anders refers to as his right-hand man. In connection with Tällbergsgården references are made to Jerk and his wife Carina and their children Claes and Josephine. The persons included in the story sustain genuine relationships described by blood and marriage, and with the inclusion of the right-hand man, mutual respect and trust (cf. Hall, 2003). The persons included maintain different management positions that dissolve into activities.

The Åkerblads-Tällbergsgården story, moreover, illustrates that hotel business activities re-enact ancestral trails through the Åkerblads and the Tällbergsgården building and land materials and other materials. The Åkerblad pedigree is traceable to the fifteenth century, wounding its way through 22 generations with the three young daughters of Rosanna and Elias, Celine, Isabelle and Alice, and the young son of Josephine, William, representing the 22nd generation. Information concerning the lives of previous generations is rather scarce, however. Records that contain genealogical information and start before the 1600s were destroyed in a fire. The records were kept in the Leksand church that burnt down in 1629 (Åkerblad, 2008).

'THE FUTURE IS IN HISTORY'

Keeping alive the history of earlier generations of the Åkerblad family is a leitmotif applied throughout present future-oriented hotel business activities. The Åkerblads website (2020) emphasizes: 'The future is in history.' Graphic representation of Åkerblads applies a distinctive mark, representing a past associated with a farming life. As a result of digital and print advertising, the old mark has become a logo and a trademark that convey the idea that the future is in history as Marketing Manager Fredrik Svedberg (personal communication, 28 August 2019) points out.

Maintenance and reconstruction of old buildings echo the voices of the Åkerblad ancestors. In the process of refurbishment one is very keen on not letting the new overshadow the old. The old–new integration allows the present to re-actualize a past. Anders Åkerblad (personal communication, 27 August 2019) comments: 'We try to keep our buildings in good shape. At the same time it is imperative to preserve the qualities that have been developed over centuries and have contributed to the distinctiveness of Åkerblads.' His son-in-law Elias Granat Åkerblad too contributes to making the old come alive through activities focused on maintenance of building and land materials. Elias (personal communication, 28 August 2019) accentuates the 'powerful force' exerted by the high-quality wood utilized in the construction of buildings hundreds of years ago and acknowledges also trees, long-lived in the courtyard:

> Parts of the buildings are very old, five or six hundred years, and are still remaining intact. The wood is in extremely good condition, close to new. A pear tree grows on an area of land in front of the oldest building. It has survived for several hundred years. There is also an apple tree, probably four or five hundred years old ... Many generations have passed ...

The year 1410 incised on the roof of a root cellar, and records of genealogical work dating back to the year 1630 presented on the walls in the main hotel building, are indicative of paths trailed by people involved in farming but also in other activities such as carpentry. Before being integrated as a wine cellar, the root cellar functioned as a carpenter workshop where Anders and Jerk Åkerblad's great-grandfather Anders Persson Åkerblad (in the following only the family name Åkerblad will be used)

(1869–1946), a skilled furniture craftsman, spent much time. More than 600 years ago, the cooler basement of a home served as a root cellar for storing food. Using the earth's thermal mass it provided a moderate temperature, reducing exposure to heat in the summer and cold in the winter (Neverman, 2020). Anders Åkerblad's workshop was equipped with a soapstone stove on which a pot was placed for heating glue and throughout the entire day it was made accessible for woodwork projects. The stove is now moved to another location close to the restaurant kitchen (Åkerblad, 2008).

Hotel business activities of the present day remind us of activities of a past primarily oriented towards farming. Under the name of Gatugården we are introduced to those activities, interwoven with building and land materials. Gatugården, which literally means 'the house by the road', refers to activities performed in, through, between and around buildings that surround a closed square yard (Åkerblad, 2008, p. 3).

A GATUGÅRDEN PAST: FARMING ACTIVITIES

Long before the name 'Åkerblads' was introduced in association with hotel, restaurant and spa, the name 'Gatugården' was used and its residents were called the Gatu family. The name 'Gatu' is put before the family name for direct descendants of the family. As Gatugården was 'the first and largest farm of the village it has brought forth several local judges, assessors and also members of the Swedish parliament. Many also were sent to fight and died in Sweden's wars on the continent', submits Christina Åkerblad (2008, p. 33). The farming Gatu family was confronted with and conquered many challenges.

In times of increasing demands for feed for the cattle the so-called *fäbod* was utilized; a small-scale farm often shared by several farmers to which cows and goats were brought, especially during the summer months when fresh green pastures awaited at the *fäbod* (Tällbergs Byalag, 2007). There were 'fäbod districts' with enormous pastures, making a square kilometre pasture available for an average of ten cows to graze on (Frödin, 1925).

Kersti Åkerblad (1864–1948), the wife of Anders Åkerblad and the great-grandmother of Anders and Jerk, was only eight years old when she did her first long distance walk of 30 kilometres in a day. A group of women left Tällberg a couple of weeks before midsummer and returned by the end of August or at the beginning of September. Kersti (in Åkerblad, 2008, p. 70) tells how days and evenings were spent at the *fäbod*:

> Every day we spent time with our cattle outside in the woods. In the evenings we gathered in one of the cottages by the open fireplace, doing craft works. Watching the flames we told legends and cock-and-bull stories. There was also much singing and playing, many women could blow cow horn trumpet and play the guitar. We really enjoyed the summer weeks and when autumn came we headed home with red rosy cheeks glowing of health.

A large quantity of cheese and butter were to be produced at the *fäbod* for the farming family to live on in the winter (Frödin, 1925). The seasonal movement of cattle continued until the beginning of the 1900s (Tällbergs Byalag, 2007). Documents from the nineteenth century also acknowledge that to get through difficult times people looked for jobs in neighbouring villages, in the city of Stockholm, located about 300 kilometres southeast of Tällberg, and overseas, in America (Åkerblad, 2008).

Christina Åkerblad (2008) tells about hardships people endured and their perseverance in the face of challenging life situations to survive and thrive. At the end of the nineteenth century, Gatugården residents were Jonas Olsson, his wife Karin and their four children Anders, Johan, Anna and Erik. In 1884, Jonas died, only 34 years old. Karin and the four children, who were all under five years at the time of the death of their father, continued to engage in farming life with the support of Karin's parents-in-law and Jonas's eldest sister. We are informed that Karin also worked as a butcher and took care of slaughtering for neighbouring farmers. Her son Erik emigrated to America and made a living by working as a tailor, making clothes to fit Hollywood film stars. At the age of nine months Erik fell out of his cradle and broke his left arm. With no possibility of having orthopaedic surgery the arm was left to self-heal and as a consequence it became shorter than the right arm. Tasks that required muscular strength in both arms were difficult to undertake for Erik. Instead, an uncle offered him training as a tailor.

Eventually Karin moved to a village near to Tällberg. Her sister-in-law Kersti (the eldest sibling of Jonas Olsson) was supposed to be shouldering the responsibility for Gatugården farming. The intended successor expressed hesitancy in taking on such a great responsibility so the decision was made by lottery to give the six siblings of Jonas an equal chance of becoming successor. As it happened, Kersti got the lottery ticket that was marked with successor but she refused to accept this result. A new lottery drawing was held and yet again Kersti got the successor ticket.

Then the matter was settled. Not repudiating the result, she uttered: 'This must be the meaning of God' (Åkerblad, 2008, p. 11). Kersti and her husband Anders Åkerblad engaged in Gatugården farming activities which were extended into guest home activities.

GUEST HOME ACTIVITIES GAINING FOCUS

Kersti and Anders Åkerblad raised four children, Alma, Maria, Anders and Gunnar. When growing up the children, representing the 18th generation, all involved in Gatugården activities which at the beginning of the 1900s included both farming and guest home activities. Eventually guest home activities gained enhanced focus. As mentioned earlier (Chapter 1), infrastructural changes in the form of railroads facilitated communications between Stockholm and Tällberg. The number of tourists increased steadily and farmhouses were converted into guest homes and hotels. Tourists also arrived by car in Tällberg and some bought land and built houses. The arrival of Professor Gösta Mittag-Leffler in a red sports car even marked the beginning of a new era, according to Christina Åkerblad (2008, p. 35):

> A new era began when the wealthy and illustrious mathematician and businessman professor Gösta Mittag-Leffler came to Tällberg with his family and entire household in May 1908. Tällberg had recently become a popular tourist resort, known for its local folklore. There were already a few small hotels and boarding-houses, but they only kept open in summers. Mittag-Leffler bought land to build a house that later was to become Hotel Dalecarlia. While it was built, he wanted to stay all the year in Tällberg and with family and servants put up at Gatugården ... The Gatu family had to move out, and its men and boys took part in building the professor's house, while its women and girls served the professor and his family ... More fun for the Gatu children was when the professor took them for a ride in his red sports car, which frightened the beasts of the still very rural village.

In 1918, a guest home was opened with 20 rooms made available for booking and full board offered for 3 SEK per day. In those days, during the winter, the women working at the guest home got up early in the morning, dressed in folk costume, lit a fire in the tile stove in the guest rooms before the guests got up and then brought them breakfast (Åkerblad, 2008).

Sadly, Alma, the eldest daughter of Kersti and Anders, died at the age of 31. Maria, the sister of Alma, married building contractor Edwin Skoglund and moved to Stockholm. The two brothers Anders and Gunnar and their wives-to-be, Elsa Axelsson and Maith Bruhn, lived in Tällberg most of their lives, engaging with guest home activities. Gunnar entertained the guests and also provided them with taxicab services using his own Chevrolet Coupé. For a year, Elsa and Anders lived in Stockholm where Anders worked as a carpenter. In 1929, their son Arne was born, a member of the 19th generation of the Åkerblad family (Åkerblad, 2008). In 1955, Arne met Christina Wallmo, his future wife.

Christina Wallmo Arrives in Tällberg

In 1955, a young woman with the name Christina Wallmo arrived in Tällberg. Christina, born in 1936, came from Gävle, a town situated approximately 140 kilometres southeast of Tällberg. In Tällberg she attended textile courses at Klockargården and worked in the Klockargården handicraft shop. After having spent two weeks in Tällberg, she met Arne Åkerblad. They married in 1957 (Christina Åkerblad, personal communication, 3 December 2020).

Arne and Christina had two sons, Anders, born in 1959, and Jerk in 1961. Their sons were encouraged to do whatever they wanted, make their own decisions and form creative ideas. Anders and Jerk chose to pursue restaurant and hotel education. Anders (personal communication, 8 October 2020) reveals:

> It all began at the age of eleven; with the help of a friend I painted the hotel buildings red. When growing up I used to spend my summer holidays doing different types of jobs, mowing the lawn, for example, and just as my grandfather did, I served as caretaker.

At an early age, Jerk (personal communication, 2 December 2020) showed an interest in food and cooking and often spent time with Hilma in the hotel kitchen. Hilma Sjöberg came from Stockholm. She was the favourite cook of Professor Mittag-Leffler, and in 1912 she accompanied him to Tällberg where he was settling down with his family. Hilma held the position as Kitchen Manager at Åkerblads for 58 years (Åkerblad, 2009).

ENTWINING WITH HOTEL BUSINESS ACTIVITIES

Guest home activities extended into hotel business activities with which Arne Åkerblad, his wife Christina and their two sons Anders and Jerk entwined. Christina helped in the kitchen, working as a cook a couple of days a week, and Arne, trained at the Hasselbacken restaurant school in Stockholm, involved in all kinds of kitchen and restaurant activities. Also their son Jerk from a young age liked to help in the kitchen. In addition, Christina sewed curtains and table cloths and decorated the rooms with flowers. At midsummer in June she picked buttercups that were woven into wreaths and crowns and placed on cabinets where they were kept to dry to be used as decoration throughout the year until next midsummer. In the autumn she picked leaves and made beautiful bouquets, placing the stems in a glycerine solution to retain the colour and texture of the leaves (Åkerblad, 2009).

For a period of time, Maith, who was married to Arne's Uncle Gunnar, worked alongside Christina and Arne. In 1970, Christina and Arne acquired Maith and Gunnar's shares of Åkerblads and became the principal owners. Also under the regime of Christina and Arne and with the support of Arne's parents Elsa and Anders and other members of the family, reconstruction projects of walls, ceilings and house sections as well as extensions of old Gatugården buildings were undertaken. Christina (Åkerblad, 2008) tells that the old farmhouse was integrated with the main hotel building. It includes a kitchen department, several guest rooms, a bridal suite and the so-called *Arstugu*, which in the past offered rooms for different categories of visitors. The Arstugu was divided into three zones by rods that hung from the ceiling. The first zone was reserved for beggars, the second for friends and acquaintances and the third for wanted persons. Fugitives who tried to hide from law enforcement were given shelter if the owner of the farm granted them permission.

Next to the main building is a pub, previously a two-storey cottage called *Lisstugu*. The first floor provided temporary accommodation for the young mistress of the house (a title used for the head of the household) when having a baby and for enjoying peace and quietness with her newborn. The staircase leading from the ground floor to the first floor was very narrow which made visitors extremely rare. Christina Åkerblad (2008) adds that it was difficult for the pregnant woman to climb the staircase and therefore she needed some assistance to push her body up stair after stair. After giving birth and having spent some time on the first floor, she became thinner and did just fine all on her own when taking the stairs. The Lisstugu, moreover, served as lodging for working girls and as scullery and office.

The present lounge and open-roofed hall on the top of the hotel lounge, the so-called *Ryggåsstugan*, was originally a threshing barn that more than 250 years ago was moved from a neighbouring village, across Lake Siljan to Tällberg. Further, there were the *Little cottage*, a house named *Gatugården* and a *härbre*, a small house built of logs laid upon one another with spaces filled with materials such as moss and mud to absorb moisture. During the late 1920s, the Little cottage, previously used as a forge, served as a private home for Anders and Elsa Åkerblad and their newborn son Arne, to later provide accommodation to staff. The house named Gatugården, where Marlene Dietrich, a German-American actress and singer spent time during World War II, was also renovated (Åkerblad, 2008).

In relatedness and closeness to materials of old Gatugården buildings, in, through, between and around which earlier Åkerblad generations trailed their paths, guest home activities extended into hotel business activities. Anders and Jerk, representing the 20th generation of the Åkerblad family, engaged in professional development activities in the form of studies and practices. However, some plans for professional development could not be implemented according to the timeline set. In 1980, Jerk was involved in a major train accident.

Professional Development

In preparation for involvement in more advanced hotel-related activities, Anders and Jerk studied at the restaurant school in Sandviken,[1] completed advanced hotel and restaurant training in Stockholm and practised at different restaurants before returning to Åkerblads. Anders (personal communication, 8 October 2020) tells:

> As a teenager I played ice hockey in the Leksand team at the level of junior hockey league but an injury put an end to hockey playing. Soon I realized there is life outside of the hockey world. My father encouraged me to study at the restaurant school in Sandviken. After finishing the studies in 1979, I practised at a restaurant on Champes Élysées in Paris. Then, I returned home for doing military service, which was made mandatory in Sweden at that time. The following three years I spent in Wiesbaden in Germany, engaging in further professional development in restaurant.

After studies at the restaurant school, and hotel and restaurant training at an advanced level, to further enhance professional development Jerk practised at two luxury restaurants in Stockholm. His plans for the future included work at a restaurant in Paris but these plans got cancelled. Jerk, then 19 years old, was involved in a train accident and it took a long time to recover from the serious injuries sustained (Jerk Åkerblad, personal communication, 2 December 2020).

A major accident occurred on 2 June in 1980, on the so-called Bergslagsbanan, about 80 kilometres south of Tällberg where two trains collided. A severe thunderstorm knocked out the railroad's signal system. The accident resulted in the death of 11 passengers, among whom were children, who had embarked on the train to enjoy a school trip. Sixty-one passengers were injured (*Dalarnas Tidningar*, 2015). Jerk Åkerblad was one of the passengers.

Anders Åkerblad (personal communication, 27 August 2019) tried to process what had happened to his brother and at the same time, engaged in growth and developmental activities:

> I saw a need for growth and development. At the beginning of the 1980s, we were seven or eight people involving in work that required shift schedules; one person started in the morning, another in the evening and as a consequence we hardly met ... I strongly felt there was a need for change and a work structure that enabled us to physically meet and interact.

In addition, Anders (personal communication, 8 October 2020) worked long hours with construction projects and all this led to a feeling of being burnt out:

> In the 1980s, experiencing anxiety after my brother's train accident and being involved in building projects and working exceptionally long hours led to a feeling of being burned out. Dealing with a builder contractor who did not meet my expectations on specified qualities, I needed to keep track on the work and helping out from seven in the morning until eleven at night, every day – seven days of the week. Physically and emotionally exhausted I was able to get some rest but it was not before long I started working again.

Yet, there was light and joy. In the 1980s, two weddings were held in Tällberg. Anders married Gunilla Sandén in 1985. Gunilla, born in 1963, came from Insjön, a neighbouring village of Tällberg. Gunilla and Anders had two daughters, Rosanna, born in 1985, and Lovisa in 1990. In 1988, Jerk married Carina Sundin. Carina, born in 1963, worked at the Åkerblads restaurant. In the marriage between Jerk and Carina, two children were born, Claes, in 1988, and Josephine in 1993. Two young families worked alongside, entwining with hotel business activities that included maintenance and reconstruction of buildings for attracting more guests and providing services that met and even exceeded guest expectations (Åkerblad, 2008, 2009).

A few years later, in 1991, there were other occasions for celebrations with visibility given to Åkerblads as a unique hotel and 'company', reflecting the Åkerblad family's hard work and professional development in hotel and restaurant activities. Åkerblads became a member of the international chain *Romantic Hotels* and of the French global association *Les Hénokiens*, presented as the second oldest family business in the world. *Les Hénokiens* welcomes a family business that has existed at least for 200 years, a bicentenary company that is in good financial health and up-to-date. The family must be owner or majority shareholder of the company, and one member of the family must hold a management position or be a member of the board. The name 'Henokiens' derives from biblical 'Enoch' (*Henok* in French), a patriarch who lived for 365 years, and without facing death ascended to Heaven (Åkerblad, 2009; *Les Hénokiens*, 2020).

In 1991, there was also a CEO shift. The CEO position unfolds activities crossed by and convergent with activities of many others with much regard continuously paid to maintenance and reconstruction.

Continuous Maintenance and Reconstruction

In 1991, quite unexpectedly a matter of succession was brought up. Arne Åkerblad was faced with the risk of going blind because of serious eye problems. The succession process speeded up and his eldest son was literally thrown into a leading position at Åkerblads. Anders, personal communication, 27 August 2019) explains:

> It was quite tough to assume leadership. I was faced with the challenge of handling business matters without my father being physically present ... We used to work together and I was always feeling confident knowing that he was the one ultimately responsible. Circumstances changed considerably as a result of my father's eye disease and he was unable to work ever again.

During the years from 1991 to 1993 Arne Åkerblad suffered repeated retinal detachments and underwent no less than 17 surgeries at the Örebro hospital, located approximately 200 kilometres south of Tällberg. Multiple times Arne was driven to the hospital by his wife, who did not exceed a speed limit of 30–40 km per hour since minimizing the amplitude of vibration was imperative. The slightest vibration would affect the retina badly (Åkerblad, 2009).

Anders Åkerblad was faced with heavy responsibility that came with the title of CEO. For him, CEO activities implied managing overall operations and making decisions without being able to discuss business matters with his father and gaining his support. At the same time, he was involved in several building projects and in the implementation of a computer system. Anders (personal communication, 8 October 2020) explains:

> Moreover, existing paper-based information and processes were digitized. To implement a computer system and converting analogue information to a digital form was quite a challenge. It proved difficult to maintain full control of the data that were transformed and it felt like I lost my footing. Again, a burned-out feeling was creeping up on me.

Without getting a long rest, once again Anders gathered strength to re-engage with work. Despite experiencing being burnt out twice he was able to stay motivated to keep on doing things, expressing a strong willingness to continue being involved in hotel business development activities. Anders (personal communication, 8 October 2020) comments:

> For many years I felt like I was balancing a slack line ... I am still suffering from tinnitus and other things and I cannot do things I used to do when I was able to juggle multiple tasks simultaneously. To relieve stress I can only deal with one or two things at a time – I have a very low threshold for stress tolerance.

The position of CEO unfolds activities that include maintenance and reconstruction of buildings and sections of buildings and further, architectural sketching. Architecture is of special interest to Anders Åkerblad. His sketches along with the final drawings of buildings account for 'the new' in integration with 'the old' and are also adjusted to fit differing opinions voiced by the members of his family. In the process of drawing and redrawing the CEO too accounts for construction standards and legal regulations that cover fire safety in and around buildings (Anders Åkerblad, personal communication, 8 October 2020). His daughter Rosanna (personal communication, 28 August 2019) highlights:

> My father became hotel owner but could have been an architect instead. All reconstruction work of old buildings is based on his drawings. He is very keen

not to push modernization too far, always integrating the new with the old. He presents us with drawings with the most innovative and smart solutions.

During the 1980s and 1990s activities were also focused on pool building. The former pool was rebuilt to serve as a bar and wine-tasting cellar, furnished with the fine carpentry works of the great-grandfather of Anders and Jerk. In 1998, on the basis of Anders's architectural design a new pool was completed. His mother Christina (Åkerblad, 2009, p. 60) describes: 'From the corridor leading to it, it looks like an old farm house with red-painted logs and old windows. There is also a glass wall and *trompe-l'oeil* paintings on the floor, emulating the garden outside.'

In 2004, geothermal heating was installed and a huge area of the Åkerblads courtyard excavated. Eleven holes were drilled, making the courtyard look like a 'war zone', notes Christina (Åkerblad, 2009, p. 101). More recent construction activities concern digital technologies and equipment. In hospitality environments there is enhanced focus on the guest room of the future with digital voice, data and video technologies emerging (Escobar, 2018). You need to adapt to the development trends that have made Wi-Fi and digital TV technology a crucial part of hotel offerings. Nowadays, health and fitness are ingrained parts of hotel offerings, which require housing spa and gym facilities and equipment. Anders Åkerblad (personal communication, 27 August 2019) acknowledges:

> Nowadays, holiday and conference guests require access to in-room free internet, and to attract and retain guests you must invest in Wi-Fi infrastructure and modify existing analogue TV systems. TV sets that run on a digital platform have been installed in all hotel rooms. We have also made big investments in spa and gym facilities and equipment. To improve guest experience we offer our guests access to spa facilities such as sauna, whirlpool and gym.

Fredrik Svedberg (personal communication, 28 August 2019) adds that the materials employed reflect the beauty of Tällberg as expressed in terms of peace and harmony:

> Tällberg is a truly beautiful place. I have lived here half my life so this place means a lot to me. It brings peace and harmony, which is also reflected in our business activities and in our use of materials, grown and made in Tällberg and in neighbouring villages. Our recent investment project regarding spa facilities employs materials such as white birch logs and slate, fine-grained metamorphic rock.

Interior design activities also promote integration between the new and the old. Rosanna Åkerblad (personal communication, 28 August 2019) explains:

> I am passionate about interior designing ... Details in the design add a special something to a building and a room. Essential for us is to preserve a sense of rootedness in the work of our ancestors, in contact with modern design trends not drifting away and forgetting about the old. It is our leitmotif, applied in all our doings and offerings. The refreshed interior of this particular building reflects the fifteenth-century farmhouse. We add modern fixtures and fresh-ness, carefully mixing the old with the new. A copper coffee pot, for example, fits the style of this hotel building that historically served as a threshing barn.

'Candles' are an indispensible part of interior design, burned to the right size before being placed in the candle holders they light the hotel build-ings with a warm glow and offer a cosy atmosphere. When growing up, Christina Åkerblad (personal communication, 3 December 2020) learned to make candles. It was a Christmas tradition in her childhood home that she maintained when coming to Åkerblads and still does. Every year she takes on the great project of making more than a thousand candles. 'When the candle-making process has been successfully completed and the freshly made candles are placed in the drying rack you are tired but at the same time, you experience a feeling of happiness', explains Christina (Åkerblad, 2009, p. 136).

The Åkerblad family entwines with various maintenance and recon-struction activities, and as the CEO (personal communication, 27 August 2019) asserts: 'It is nice to work with the family.'

'It is Nice to Work with the Family'

On a daily basis Anders interacts with his wife Gunilla, the daughters Rosanna and Lovisa, his son-in-law Elias and many others. Today, there are 45 people involved in Åkerblads hotel business activities. In the following, the focus is narrowed to people related by blood and marriage and to a relationship expressed in terms of 'right-hand man'.

Gunilla (personal communication, 3 December 2020) introduces herself as general factotum, which includes supporting and working along with the newly employed Head of Household, providing assis-tance where needed and engaging in developmental hotel activities. As the former Head of Household, Gunilla hired and trained staff, created workable schedules, oversaw and worked alongside the staff. Gunilla has also experience from being involved in reception, day-to-day and administrative office activities and from interior designing and flower decorating at festive occasions such as weddings (Gunilla Åkerblad, personal communication, 22 January 2021).

Transgressing the formality of the titles of Head of Household and CEO, we are introduced to Gunilla and Anders as parents, who raised two daughters. Becoming a mother, Gunilla was faced with the demands of combining her engagement in hotel business activities with childcare. To juggle the responsibilities of these activities and new babies, she brought the babies along to the office. When growing up Rosanna and Lovisa spent much time with their parents and grandparents in the hotel buildings. They never went to preschool. Rosanna and Lovisa were encouraged by their parents to do whatever they wanted, to follow their inner compass and make their own decisions.

Rosanna (personal communication, 28 August 2019) comments on her upbringing and refers to time spent with her grandmother Christina and to an education that focused on tourism and hotel management:

> I have never felt obligated to remain in Tällberg, restricted by my parents from doing certain things. Yet, your family may have a big influence on your interests and professional development ... I did not attend preschool, instead I spent time here with my grandmother Christina. My father and mother worked a lot. The hotel felt as my home. I used to accompany my grandmother, lighting different places in the hotel buildings with candles ... I also helped out with some restaurant, cleaning and reception jobs. After finishing primary school in Tällberg and high school in Leksand I went to Switzerland, enrolling in a three-year Bachelor programme at the International Business in Hotel and Tourism Management School. Thereafter, I moved to the United States for hotel management training at a beautiful golf resort, a venue for PGA tours. The training was rather basic, however, so after three months I returned to Tällberg ... Now, I am here to stay.

Today, Rosanna (personal communication, 28 August 2019) holds the position of Hotel Manager which implies a diverse number of activities:

> You hold a position with which comes certain duties but you are also involved in activities not defined by your position; you are everywhere ... My position implies making sure that everything works, that the department heads synchronize their doings, that invoicing are carried out correctly, etcetera. We have a chef, a restaurant manager, a kitchen manager and a reception manager, and two years ago we appointed a person responsible for conferences and events, an area of activities that previously was part of reception activities.

Today, conference and event activities are handled separately as an autonomous organization unit.

In 2002, Rosanna then 17 years old met Elias Granat, her husband to be. Elias, ice hockey player at an elite level, was also 17 years old. Now that he has finalized a career as a professional hockey player, he engages in maintaining all the buildings and gardens that go under the name of Åkerblads. He also works as a personal trainer at the Åkerblads gym. Elias (personal communication, 28 August 2019) clarifies:

> Being a hockey player means a particular way of living ... you are scheduled for intense exercises in the mornings and for hockey games in the evenings, how you spend the hours in between is up to you. Here, you stay active throughout the whole day. There is always something going on and this makes the entire day interesting and fun. And, like in hockey playing, the hotel activities require physical involvement and that is good.

Rosanna and Elias have three daughters, Celine, born in 2013, Isabelle, in 2018, and Alice, in 2019, representing the 22nd generation.

Lovisa lives in London with her boyfriend and works at a hotel that has temporally closed due to the coronavirus outbreak. She is currently visiting Tällberg, and involved in Åkerblads activities. Lovisa (personal communication, 13 January 2021) tells: 'Now I am primarily called to assist in the restaurant, which has been faced with many restrictions in connection with the corona pandemic. By the way, you could say I am a sort of general factotum, providing assistance where needed.' Moreover, Lovisa engages in activities, extended through the construction of the Åkerblads spa facilities and equipment. Her father (personal communication, 27 August 2019) comments: 'Lovisa is full of energy, willing to make a lot of changes ... of course, this is much appreciated and I recognize in her something of myself.'

After completing a two-year education programme in dermatology and spa therapy in Stockholm, Lovisa received the Cidesco Diploma, the world's most prestigious qualification for aesthetics and beauty therapy (*Qualifications Cidesco*, 2021). Moreover, she obtained a Bachelor's degree in International Hospitality Management after a four-year programme of study at Ecole Hôtelière de Lausanne in Switzerland (Lovisa Åkerblad, personal communication, 13 January 2021).

On a daily basis, Anders Åkerblad (personal communication, 8 October 2020) also interacts with his mother Christina: 'My mother and I talk about everything ... she comes here every day.' In addition to being a mother, grandmother and great-grandmother, Christina Åkerblad is one's first point of contact when calling Åkerblads to book a room. Her voice warmly welcomes you to Åkerblads, initiating interactions with many unknown others.

Although not related to the Åkerblad family by blood or marriage, Fredrik Svedberg (personal communication, 28 August 2019) has become nearly a member of the Åkerblad family:

> Many years of collaboration between me and the members of the family has fostered a close relationship characterized by mutual trust and respect. You have to respect that for the members of the family, being involved in hotel business activities is not work: it is a life. They partake in daily operations and make all decisions, concerning both short term and long term changes and investments, always paying respect for the history, which is made alive in oral and written forms, in daily talk and interactions among the members of the family. Christina Åkerblad gives talk about the history. Our conference guests appreciate very much learning about the history.

Anders Åkerblad introduces Fredrik Svedberg as his right-hand man. Fredrik, former chef and former Food and Beverage Manager responsible for all operations at the Åkerblads restaurant, assumed the position of Marketing Manager in 2010. This position entails activities that, for example, focus on the development of a graphic profile to communicate information on web pages and in print material clearly showing users what Åkerblads hotel, restaurant and spa are about. What it means to be the CEO's right-hand man, Fredrik (personal communication, 28 August 2019) comments:

> We trust and respect each other and we know each other very well; we share a deep understanding on different matters and we do not need to talk much … So, anytime Anders goes away he need not worry much ... I work together with his daughters and jointly we take care of things and keep track of what is going on.

Jerk Åkerblad, his wife Carina and their children Claes and Josephine have become increasingly involved in Tällbergsgården hotel business activities, unfolding in close relation to Åkerblads hotel business activities. Tällbergsgården, constituted by building and land materials, was acquired by the Åkerblad family in 1994.

In Association with Tällbergsgården

On the very day of Jerk Åkerblad's birthday on 3 March in 1994, the Åkerblad family received an inquiry from the president of the Leksand savings bank. Christina Åkerblad (2009, p. 29) relates:

> He was wondering if we would consider being the new owners of Tällbergsgården, which was opting for a new regime. We ruminated on that idea and came to the conclusion that it would be a great opportunity for our beloved son Jerk and his family to take care of this hotel ... In May 1994, we acquired the hotel ... There was plenty to do. This implied among other things, demolition and replacement of an old house, and improvement of finances through the creation of 25 new guest rooms.

Tällbergsgården originally served as an elementary school, in 1918 was bought by Wilhelmina and Johan Johansson who turned the school house into a hotel. The hotel was frequently visited by members of the Swedish royal family, actors, musicians, writers and painters among whom was Gustaf Ankarcrona. He fell in love with one of the daughters of the Johansson family and visited the hotel very often (Åkerblad, 2009). Ankarcrona is recognized as a pioneer of the Swedish arts and crafts movement. He saw it as imperative to promote and develop the Tällberg local character embodied in handicraft works. He built a home (*Holen*) in Tällberg, which today constitutes a historic monument (Tällbergs Byalag, 2007).

Being afforded the opportunity by the president of the Leksand savings bank to acquire Tällbergsgården was much appreciated. 'Carina and Gatu-Jerk and the children would be able to bring their own ideas to life, involving in development projects of their own interest', Christina Åkerblad (2009, p. 9) emphasized. Carina (personal communication, 27 August 2019) comments: 'We thought it was a fantastic opportunity. The location of Tällbergsgården gives you a wonderful view of Lake Siljan.' At the time of the acquisition, Carina and Jerk's son Claes was six years old and their daughter Josephine one year old.

From 1994 Carina and Jerk engaged in Tällbergsgården hotel business activities which included making improvements to the old buildings through rather extensive renovation and reconstruction work. During the ensuing year, Jerk was also involved in construction work regarding Åkerblads conference rooms but sadly, fell ill and was diagnosed with a brain tumour, most likely related to the severity of the train accident in 1980. As it turned out, the tumour was benign and Jerk underwent surgery (Åkerblad, 2009). Carina (personal communication, 27 August 2019) adds:

> The renovation work became a rather burdensome process as my husband Jerk was diagnosed with a brain tumour. We had also to take care of our little daughter Josephine ... Surgery could not remove the entire tumour, originally of a size comparable to a tennis ball. Now, monitoring tests are given routinely to check for any signs of recurrence. Fortunately my husband sees life positively and to be able to stay positive is essential, doing otherwise you might not be able to cope.

Over the years to come, Carina and Jerk were to take on several reconstruction projects. Refurbishment work focused on *Petrus Gatugården*, the annex connected with the main Tällbergsgården building. The annex, previously a school, was restored and turned into double rooms that were painted, furnished and lined with Laura Ashley textiles. Suites with open fireplaces and with bathrooms including whirlpool baths for two people were built. A new balcony, running along the renovated guest rooms on the second floor of the main building, was constructed, allowing a spectacular view of Lake Siljan. Moreover, the old coffee parlour was transformed into a reception and pub. On the basis of Jerk's idea to fill the rooms in the main building with more light, the ceiling was raised. The garden got a whirlpool for six persons and a house with a sauna (Åkerblad, 2009).

Since Tällbergsgården investments and renovations proved financially challenging, Carina and Jerk came up with the idea of introducing a new table water, *Aqua Tällberg*, and a special Tällberg ale, *Tällbers* (Jerk Åkerblad, personal communication, 7 October 2020). Practically implemented, these ideas turned out to be financially advantageous (Åkerblad, 2009).

Today, Tällbergsgården consists of eight buildings that provide 33 rooms for hotel and conference guests with about nine people involved in business-related activities. Characterized as a privately owned historic, romantic and authentic boutique hotel with charming inn and cosy guest houses, Tällbergsgården has qualified as a member of *Countryside Hotels* (Countryside Hotels Website, 2021).

Entwined with a variety of activities
In 2006 Jerk Åkerblad attainted full ownership of Tällbergsgården. His brother Anders became the sole owner of Åkerblads. As a limited company Tällbergsgården was initially run as part of the Åkerblads

concern for which Anders was ultimately responsible (Anders Åkerblad, personal communication, 8 October 2020). Today, Jerk shares the ownership of Tällbergsgården with his wife Carina. Jerk also holds the position of CEO. Their ownership is constituted of activities related to reception, kitchen, cleaning drains, changing lamps and hosting dinner, for instance. Carina (personal communication, 27 August 2019) illustrates:

> I interact a lot with the guests, providing them with daily services … I am working with a number of activities at the reception desk, making reservation for rooms, conferences, weddings and parties, and in collaboration with the restaurant manager and others ensuring that the food that comes out of the kitchen keeps a high quality and meets the nutritional needs and dietary habits of our guests. I am also taking care of flowers and doing some decorating. It is a great teamwork and much effort is put into building a good reputation for Tällbergsgården and providing a welcome familial feeling. Also, there is a big focus on food and wine, it is very important for us to offer the guests a culinary experience when staying at our hotel. Our guests are very satisfied with our services.

What the formal owner and CEO titles convey is elucidated by Jerk (personal communication, 27 August 2019):

> Well, it is everything from cleaning drains, changing lamps to being involved in cooking, hosting dinners for hotel and conference guests, being responsible for finances and having a close look at other activities while making sure that everything runs smoothly. Initially, my interest was in cooking and I was trained as a chef but like my grandfather, who was rather versatile, I enjoy doing many different things and testing new ideas and solutions. Maybe 40 days, in a common year of 365 days, are pretty calm, giving us a break and allowing us to rest and recuperate. Otherwise, there is always something to do. We must also take care of the buildings, through regulative maintenance keeping them in shape as there are many causes for decay in old buildings.

Owning and managing activities are interwoven with the activities performed by Claes and Josephine. Their father (personal communication, 2 December 2020) reveals:

> Claes has the position of Hotel Manager and like me he involves in activities such as washing dishes and cleaning drains. Josephine focuses on accounting. She takes care of all invoices and keeps records of financial transactions, also pointing out to me where savings can be done.

Jerk, Carina, Claes and Josephine are immersed in a variety of Tällbergsgården hotel business activities. 'Tällbergsgården does not define a job or a company but a home and a way of life', highlights Jerk (personal communication, 27 August 2019). The activities are caught up with building and land materials that create a wonderful work environment as Carina (personal communication, 27 August 2019) conveys:

> It is not a modern hotel; it is a beautiful little cosy hotel that is characterized by an intimate and warm atmosphere that creates a homely feeling ... when looking out of the window, the scenery that appears in front of my eyes is like a painting, and ever shifting.

By Lake Siljan in Tällberg, Åkerblads and Tällbergsgården dissolve into hotel business activities that define a life. As Christina Åkerblad (2008, p. 106), the mother of Anders and Jerk, summarizes: 'Running a hotel together is a way of living, twenty-four hours a day.' This way of living extends through building and land materials and other materials that echo the voices of people now long gone.

A COMMENT

The Åkerblads-Tällbergsgården story illustrates business activities with which members of the Åkerblad family and others presently entwine, indicating that a past, stretching back more than 600 years, according to traditional calendar time, is intimately interwoven with the present with sights on a future. We recognize an open-ended present that sparks a repetition of the old in integration with the new. A story plot that linearly covers 22 generations cannot be identified. 'Past' implies a living historicizing process that mediates through old building and land materials and other materials used by the ancestors, suggesting closeness rather than remoteness in relation to those presently engaging in maintenance and reconstruction, which seem to be the predominant Åkerblads and Tällbergsgården activities. A past does not come down to members of the Åkerblad family and others as a single separate whole referred to as a tradition of importance to preserve and maintain in the present (cf. Bakhtin, 1981; Spence, 1982). As beings-in-the-world, people move in between present actualities and future possibilities with historicizing occurring along their *Daseins* (Chapter 3) as Heidegger (1962) expresses it.

The Åkerblads-Tällbergsgården story directs attention to materials that mainly relate to buildings and land. The material, in interwovenness with the social, constituted of human interactions and genuine relations, relates to spatiality, further discussed with regard to *existential space* and *bodily lived place* in the last chapter (Chapter 8).

NOTE

1.   Sandviken is situated about 120 km southeast of Tällberg.

8. An alternative approach to family business

In complementing existing research of family business the book proposes an alternative approach – a theory of socio-material weaving, informed by the philosophical tradition of hermeneutic phenomenology with the existential phenomenon of *Dasein* designating our being-in-the-world, a being that we share with others. Five stories, the Siljanstrand, Siljansgården, Green Hotel, Klockargården and the Åkerblads-Tällbergsgården story, direct our attention to business activities caught up in materials that relate to spatiality as expressed by existential space and bodily lived place. As pointed out in this chapter, the hermeneutic-phenomenological concepts of *Dasein*, mood, care, circumspection and significance direct us to existential space, and the geography- and anthropology-related concepts of tenacity and subjection, concerned with the placilizing of the human body, and the concept of landscape with reference to a shaped land, direct us to bodily lived place. Space and place are aspects of a hermeneutic-phenomenological *Dasein*, transcending a duality relationship. A study that advances a hermeneutic-phenomenological understanding of the social in relation to the spatial material shifts the focus away from a systems-oriented conception of family business.

The chapter also acknowledges that theory building is a complicated task. Qualitative researchers employ different methods and there is no consensus on what theory is. A theory of socio-material weaving directs attention to activities, constituted of the sociality of human interactions and relations, interwoven with the material. Ontologically embracing a hermeneutic-phenomenological being-in-the-world view that foregrounds our entwinement with activity in amongst materials, it brings existential space and bodily lived place to the fore. As noted, under the name of Tällberg, we realize that place in its bodily lived extension implies a continuous *taking in* through the activities with which people entwine.

EXISTENTIAL SPACE

Five stories allow family business in the forms of hotel, guest home and school to dissolve into activities, enmeshed with materials spatially constituted and extended. Little interest is paid to hotel, guest home and school as legal entities set up as limited companies to be owned and managed, and as systems with a distinction drawn between family and business and between the internal and the external. As the stories demonstrate, owner, CEO and managerial positions unfold owning and managing activities, seamlessly flowing into other business-oriented activities caught up in materials. The activities with which people are entwined bring the social and the material together. The social refers to human interactions and relations, and the material to things primarily associated with buildings and land, and these things are ascribed a *being*. The hermeneutic-phenomenological assumption of being-in-the-world embraces a *Dasein* that also shows sensitivity to a being of the material (Chapter 3).

Materials can be thought of as tools (or equipment), that is, as being towards something, from a present-at-hand to a readiness-to-hand, which implicates a move from theoretical to practical significance (Heidegger, 1962). Assigned theoretical significance, the materials imply a nexus of possibilities of use in activity. The materials respond to the question of how far or near they are from acquiring significance in practice (Schatzki, 2010) which has nothing to do with physical proximity and distance. The possibility of being useful attributes theoretical significance to the mate-rial and when actually used the material, in its 'toolness' as one might say, or 'equipmentality' as Heidegger (1962) expresses it, gains practical significance, spatially extending business activity with which people are entwined, affording existential space. People find themselves within activities in the existential sense of being 'immersed in the accommoda-tions of practical concerns' (Lamprou, 2017, p. 1737).

A being-in-the-world carries with it affective mood, which stamped with care means being sensitive to, responsive to and reflective of emerg-ing circumstances (Schatzki, 2010). Like atmosphere, mood is already there, disclosing the world to us (Ciborra, 2006). Affective mood has a stamp of care which suggests encountering the world in solicitude with others as pronounced in terms of circumspective engagement with the world (Heidegger, 1962). In care, conditioned by this mood, existential space is promoted through translating theoretical significance to practical significance (Chapter 3).

The Siljanstrand story, closely linked to the Siljansgården and the Green Hotel story, and the Klockargården and the Åkerblads-Tällbergsgården story illustrate business activities *with* materials. Care, mood, circumspection, theoretical and practical significance (as presented above) contribute an understanding of existential space. Since these concepts refer to the unobservable we are only left with indications. Present future-oriented activities are reflections of a mood that in association with care attunes people and makes certain materials matter to them. When engaging materials with activities, in their beings of equipmentality recognizing a move from a present-at-hand to a ready-to-hand (from theoretical to practical significance), we can assume existential space to be implied in a human's changed way of being in relation to material. A changed way of being can be concretized through the extension, focus and refocusing of business activities with which people as beings-in-the-world entwine.

In Association with Siljanstrand, Siljansgården and Green Hotel

The Siljanstrand story refers to Hans Erik Börjeson and Mats Blomqvist, whose respective positions as owner and property manager unfold business activities that direct much attention to renewal and development of building and land materials. The story offers glimpses of their close relationship and their interactions regarding a great many building projects. Arguably, it is in care they picked up what aspects of a building project were relevant for the purpose of converting the Siljansgården guest home buildings into hotel Siljanstrand buildings, which also included improvements to land materials. Care in its primordial connection with mood as reflected by 'cultural achievement' implicates circumspective engagement with the Siljansgården building and land materials, which materials, admittedly, served as tools for the extension of business activities in relation to 'hotel'.

Börjeson and Blomqvist are not separated from renewal and development activities; they find themselves in activities – in the existential sense of being immersed, practically appropriating materials in activities. It can be contended that existential space is enacted through a move from theoretical significance attributed the materials, to practical significance achieved through the use of the materials, to offer the hotel guests 'culture, beauty and history'. The story refers to, for example, timbered houses, belfry, pebble walls, rose beds, soil and apple trees, assigned practical significance for the extension of business activities, suggesting a web of significances. The social, constituted by the interactions and close relationship between Börjeson and Blomqvist, is interwoven with the material.

The Siljansgården story refers to land material employed by Signe Bergner for building a home; a vacant piece of Tällberg land rendered theoretical significance. Harald Alm enmeshed in the home building activities. Presumably, the passionate love between Signe and Harald intimated a mode of mood which imprinted with care made them attuned and committed to home building materials, ascribed practical significance. In the move from theoretical to practical significance, existential space is delineated. Further, the Siljansgården story tells that business activities focused on sports, recreation and education, constituted of interactions between Signe Bergner, Harald Alm, school children and co-workers. The activities were strongly oriented towards renewal and development of building and land materials. After the death of Signe, Harald continued to build in cooperation with his second wife Berit Ejder, and after her death in cooperation with Annedore Keil with business activities more geared towards guest home lodging. Existential space is promoted through the translation of theoretical significance to practical significance of materials used in the building and development projects these couples and others engaged with. The story refers to materials such as grass, rose bushes, birch trees, old mill, timber and Chinese fabrics. Assigned practical significance for the extension of business activities a web of significances is constituted. It can be contended that care was conditioned by a mood that allowed business activities to happen to make the ideas of a holistic treatment of body and soul, and a 'co-worker for Life' come alive. When faced with sorrows and challenges much effort was put into continuing working. Grieving his first wife's death, Harald Alm uttered: 'My grief became my work.' The sociality of business activities is interwoven with materials related to buildings and land. Land is described by 'a sloping terrain where terraces were built and where lawns were bordered by beautiful stone walls and hedges'.

After the death of Harald Alm, his daughter Signe, his son Bertil, his grandchild Olof and others engaged in guest home lodging activities. Already from a young age, Signe, Bertil and Olof were involved in various activities that extended through practically significant materials associated with the Siljansgården buildings and land, constituting existential space. Olof specifically refers to activities interlinked with food materials. In 2010, due to changing circumstances Siljansgården was sold at auction, and Signe and Olof no longer were provided relatedness and closeness to the Siljansgården building and land materials. With reference to Signe, there is an indication of an alteration in mood with *Dasein* veiled by feelings of sadness experienced when forced to leave Siljansgården as reflected by her dream to return to Siljansgården.

As indicated by the Green Hotel story, business activities, constituted of interactions between Hans Erik Börjeson and others, engaged building and land materials and also other materials such as glass and paintings. The social and the material were brought together such as existential space was promoted. Admittedly, Börjeson attributed the hotel theoretical significance when encountered in its material exposition on the top of the hill he climbed together with his friends. In view of the possibility to make the dream of creating a San Michele come true, the hotel served as a theoretical significant tool. However, it took 12 years before practical significance was enacted since it was through the acquisition, renewal and development of the hotel that Börjeson's dream materialized. Practical significance developed when materials were utilized for making more rooms available for hotel guests, providing staff housing, constructing a terrace and a swimming pool with underwater sound system and a descendible glass roof, and building a room for exhibiting art works. A web of practical significances is constituted of materials such as hill, *härbre*, glass floor, old houses and art works. It can be contended that the ways in which the owner in owning activities cared about the Green Hotel building and land materials unfolded according to a mood that in association with the San Michele dream attuned him to the material. Existential space is implied in the from-towards movement of theoretical and practical significance.

In Association with Klockargården

The Klockargården story reveals that a little deserted cottage, beautifully and centrally located in Tällberg by the thoroughfare, attracted the interest of the young couple Astrid and August Sandberg who were searching for a home of their own. Care, conditioned by mood as reflected by their intention to make a life for themselves and engaging in business activities, arguably attuned them to the cottage and road materials. Projecting usability, the materials gained theoretical significance and when actually used practical significance, suggesting existential space. The cottage material served as a tool that in relation to its location as described in terms of road material enabled home building but also the extension of handicraft shop, bakery and café activities to earn money. Building and land materials were relevant for the Sandberg couple, their interactions and relations with their children, Kerstin, Gudrun, Lars, Per and Margareta, when at different time periods attending to sheep farming, textile education, guest home and hotel business activities. Sheep wool was used for weaving, knitting and sewing textiles. In anticipation of producing fine handicraft items, the 250 sheep ascribed to theoretical significance and when wool was used the sheep admittedly gained practical significance. The existential space promoted is reflected in fine textile activity extension. In addition, the sheep took care of the view of Lake Siljan, attributed practical significance when grazing the growing grass and in that sense contributing to existential space, allowing people to enjoy a great view of the lake.

The owner and CEO positions held by Astrid and August's son Per (from the 1960s to the beginning of the 2000s) unfolded owning and managing activities that extended through timbered houses, cottages and *härbren*, many of which were bought, dismantled, moved from other places in Dalarna and rebuilt on the Klockargården land. Also paintings, tapestries and folk costume materials and nostalgic things were encountered circumspectively, assigned importance for a life not detached from business activities as Per Sandberg admitted. Materials are not only present-at hand but also ready-to-hand, their beings offering existential space through a move from theoretical to practical significance. The story indicates that it is in care, conditioned by mood expressed in terms of a wholeness that makes material things in close association with nature, art and nostalgia highly relevant to the extension of business activities. Materials, assigned practical significance for the extension of business activities, are constitutive of a web of significances.

Inger, the wife of Per Sandberg, engaged in designing, weaving, sewing and decorating activities. Not only implementing certain designs and doing things *to* textile material, she worked *with* and brought the material into being. There is a thing-being that does not separate Inger from the material, promoting existential space through the translation of theoretical significance to practical significance. Not conceived of as an empty space that needed to be filled with textile materials in the form of curtains, cloths and bed covers, the rooms admittedly *became* as Inger in entwinement with textile activities responded to the spatiality of the Klockargården buildings and rooms, composing, and promoting existential space.

When struck down by sorrow at the death of his son Lars and his wife Inger it would have been easy for Per Sandberg to be led astray in a mood with *Dasein* veiled by feelings of sadness and despair and loss of interest in hotel business activities. Yet, in interactions with his son Anders and daughter-in-law Susanna he continued being involved in hotel business activities that were extended with enhanced focus on entertainment and conferences. In 2019, when owning and managing activities became the entwinement of Staffan Malmqvist, presented as the new and sole owner of the Klockargården shares, Per Sandberg engaged with the Bergbacken project with business activities making land material available for presumptive buyers who wish to build a home in Tällberg and enjoy a beautiful view of Lake Siljan. Today, Anders Sandberg is also bound up in Bergbacken activities. Being present-at-hand, the Bergbacken land is assigned theoretical significance. Being ready-to-hand and effectuated in actual activities, the land material is attributed practical significance in the constitution of existential space.

As the Klockargården story indicates, the social and the material are interwoven. Members of the five-generation Sandberg family, the wife of Per Sandberg and the wife of Anders Sandberg entwined with a variety of business activities, extending through the Klockargården building and land materials and other materials.

In Association with Åkerblads and Tällbergsgården

The Åkerblads-Tällbergsgården story refers to hotel business activities that unfold through materials associated with houses, cottages and *härbren* anchored to the Åkerblads and the Tällbergsgården land. The owner and CEO positions of Anders Åkerblad dissolve into owning and managing activities constituted of interactions with his mother Christina, his wife Gunilla, his daughters Rosanna and Lovisa, his son-in-law Elias and his right-hand man Fredrik. This suggests that owning and managing activities are crisscrossed by activities focused on marketing, household heading, hotel managing, restaurant, spa and gym training and on keeping building and land materials in good shape. Also the owner and CEO position of Jerk Åkerblad unfold through activities that flow into activities in which his wife Carina, his son Claes and his daughter Josephine are enmeshed. Owning and managing activities include cleaning drains, changing lamps, cooking, hosting dinners for hotel and conference guests and recording financial transactions while 'making sure that everything runs smoothly'. The owner position of Carina entails reception activities, room, conference, weddings and party bookings, decorating, and activities that relate to collaboration with the restaurant manager for ensuring that food is kept to a high quality. In this crisscrossing of business activities there is a substantial focus on the integration of old material with new material.

Present future-oriented hotel business activities re-actualize a past that tells about farming and other activities with which members of earlier generations of the Åkerblad family were entwined. This past unfolds in, between, through and around the old Gatugården buildings and the *fäbod*. In sensitivity and responsiveness to changing circumstances (Schatzki, 2010) regarding the increasing stream of tourists in Tällberg, farming activities extended into guest home and hotel business activities that engaged Gatugården building and land materials, and from the 1990s, Tällbergsgården building and land materials. The three-section Arstugu, the Lisstugu with its narrow staircase, the threshing barn called Ryggåsstugan, the Little cottage that previously was used as a forge, and the old school building, Petrus Gatugården, echo what members of earlier generations and others attended to. The buildings exemplify 'the old', circumspectively encountered and attuned to in the present. In relation to the old materials, future possibilities of attracting more hotel and conference guests are projected, assigning theoretical significance to the old. The story demonstrates that the old buildings are relevant for adding newness in the forms of Wi-Fi and digital TV technology, spa and gym facilities, geothermal heating, for raising a ceiling, constructing a cosy pub, indoor and outdoor pools and a sauna, and complementing rooms and suites with open fireplaces, whirlpool baths and balconies. Maintenance and reconstruction activities contribute a readiness-to-hand through the attribution of practical significance to the old building materials, delineating existential space.

Maintenance and reconstruction activities are interlinked with architectural and interior design activities that make use of materials such as timber, birch logs, soapstone, flowers, glass, fine-grained metamorphic rock and candle wax, constituting a web of practical significances. The Åkerblads and the Tällbergsgården buildings and rooms *become* as architectural and design activities respond to the spatiality of them. Of theoretical and practical significance, the materials contribute existential space, enabling hotel business activities to extend to offering holiday and conference guests a comfortable and enjoyable stay, and meeting and even exceeding their wishes and requirements.

Present future-oriented maintenance, reconstruction, architectural and interior design activities entail a redefinition of the material such as the material allows anew for serviceability, conduciveness and usability in activities. Familiar with earlier generations' farm-related activities, old materials are encountered with concern and integrated with the new, affording existential space. In care, conditioned by mood as reflected by circumspective concern for activities caught up in materials associated with the Åkerblads and the Tällbergsgården buildings and land that echo the voices of members belonging to earlier generations of the Åkerblad family and other voices, present hotel business activities are given direction towards a future. Activities proceed along paths threaded by people not living any longer, adding something new to the old. We can imagine long chains of interchanging theoretical and practical significances widening through more than 600 years with people contemplating continuously the use of materials and, depending on circumstances, constructing ways to appropriate materials in activities.

It is important to note that *Dasein*'s spatialization, as described above in terms of existential space with reference to the five stories, is also of bodily nature. Materials serve as tools ready-to-hand for bodily use (Heidegger, 1962). Moreover, the bodily gains place-related expressions. Body is what links the human 'to lived place in its sensible and perceptible features', purports Casey (2001, p. 683). Place is bodily experiential exploration (cf. Lefebvre, 1991). With place in focus we open up to the bodily lived and with the notion of *lived* we continue to account for an ongoing integrative life process through which the individual as a being-in-the-world relates to the Other and to a past (Chapter 3). In the book, space and place are aspects of a hermeneutic-phenomenological *Dasein*, transcending a duality relationship in the appreciation of a material space- and place-related extension in business activities with which people entwine. Space with emphasis on the existential, and place with emphasis on the bodily lived are integrated through the focus on the social and the material and their interwovenness.

BODILY LIVED PLACE

A human being encounters place by going out to meet it and by coming in to it and getting to know it (Casey, 2001). The incoming implies placilizing the human body which accounts for tenacity and subjection. Tenacity concerns the impression we gain of coming in to a place and the lasting effect it has, and subjection '*what we are as an expression of the way place is'* in all its idiosyncrasies (Casey, 2001, p. 688, emphasis in original). The five stories do not provide much information on Tällberg in its idiosyncrasies. It is rather with reference to Siljanstrand, Siljansgården, Green Hotel, Klockargården and Åkerblads-Tällbergsgården we get a sense of the Tällberg place, made present in hotel, guest home and school business activities immersed with materials that impress themselves on the human body.

The Siljansgården, the Green Hotel and the Klockargården story indicate that Signe Bergner, Hans Erik Börjeson, Astrid and August Sandberg were left with a strong impression when coming in to Tällberg, with the lasting effects of their incomings affording a bodily placilizing. Signe Bergner reached out to and came in to Tällberg, searching for a piece of land for building a home of her own. Land material in the form of a hill, grading off to Lake Siljan with groves, grass fields, stone walls, juniper and rose bushes, and birch trees seemed to matter to her immediately, promoting bodily placilizing. Hans Erik Börjeson was unexpectedly exposed to materials associated with the Green Hotel and with the hill at the top of which the hotel is situated. When listening to his colourful description of the scenery that met his eyes we understand bodily placilizing as an intense experience. What it felt to be in the Tällberg place and walking up the steep hill of Green Hotel describes a presence compressed in his wish to buy the hotel or build a similar hotel. For Astrid and August Sandberg the little deserted cottage, beautifully located alongside the public road in Tällberg, meant bodily placilizing, indicating a way forward – towards home building and engagement in business activities. Moreover, the Klockargården story acknowledges that for Inger Sandberg (Astrid and August Sandberg's daughter-in-law) the coming in to Tällberg meant the construction of opportunity for enrolment in Klockargården textile education. As the Åkerblads-Tällbergsgården story reveals, also for Christina Åkerblad bodily placiziling in Tällberg relates to involvement in textile education.

The lasting impressions of coming in to Tällberg, arguably, contributed to the incomers' habitation. The incomers became Tällberg inhabitants, bodily placilized they carried on a life in entwinement with a variety of business activities, working with and weaving in amongst materials (cf. Ingold, 2011). Habitation, as opposed to occupation of a place, implicates place as a lived world that develops, extends and regenerates through inhabitants' activities (Chapter 3). Place is 'energized and transformed by the bodies that belong to it' (Casey, 2001, p. 688). Described as land*scape*, place defines a world of materials formed through human muscular activity and with the assistance of animals. The *scaped* and lived place is *with* us when new paths are threaded in connection with paths made in a past. The human body works 'with materials and with the land, "sewing itself in" to the textures of the world along the pathways of sensory involvement' (Ingold, 2011, p. 133).

Past Paths Crossed in the Present

The stories elicit that present future-oriented business activities connect with a past. The Hotel Siljanstrand story prompts a past to come alive with reference to the Siljansgården story. 'Cultural achievement', constitutive of a bunch of activities with which Hans Erik Börjeson and Mats Blomqvist entwined enmeshed with building and land materials, recalls paths trailed by Harald Alm, his wives and others. Signe Bergner and Harald Alm built a home bodily engaging with materials such as timber, stone, grass and Chinese fabrics. They moved stones, raised fences and prepared lawns for leisure and sports activities. Home building activities extended into school activities, the primary intention of which was to integrate body and soul. School activities were carried out as school children and 'co-workers for Life' muscularly engaged with building and land materials. When encumbered with sorrows and faced with challenges that risked interrupting school-related activities, even agency was assigned to the Siljansgården land as reflected by Alm's words: 'In spring greenery I heard the ground crying.'

Signe Alm, her brother Bertil and her son Olof were already placilized. The Siljansgården describes a world they shared with their parents and co-workers. As Tällberg inhabitants and beings-in-the-Siljansgården-world they followed the paths scaped and drawn by their predecessors Harald Alm, Signe Bergner, Berit Ejder and later on, Annedore Keil, who bodily hacked and scratched into a piece of the Tällberg earth.

The Green Hotel story informs about building and land materials that in a past constituted the so-called Flower Hotel. The path threaded by Ninnie and Börje Green was followed and crossed in the present with sights on the future when Hans Erik Börjeson and others immersed themselves in renewal and development activities. Börjeson lets us even hear the sound of the swinging axes that added log to log as when the ancestors built for themselves and their descendants.

The Klockargården story mentions the Tänger house and its threshing floor where farmers thrashed grains for centuries, the old mill brought from the shore of the Dal River and 'Fejset', an old cowshed with a stone wall including a piece of a meteorite that hit earth 377 million years ago. Paths are trailed by members of the five-generation Sandberg family and today, by the new owner Staffan Malmqvist, who also shows a great sensitivity to old materials. The Åkerblads-Tällbergården story informs about old buildings that remind us of Gatugården farming activities dating back to the 1400s. With Ingold (2011, p. 126) it can be assumed that the farmers scaped the Gatugården land 'with foot, axe and plough, and with the assistance of their domestic animals, trod, hacked and scratched their lines into the earth'.

People inhabit a place in interactions with one another, recovering and transforming materials such as soil, wood, and materials produced by cows, goats and sheep. Members of the 20th and 21st generation of the Åkerblad family, already placilized, but not place-bound, carry on their lives, making paths that suggest bodily involvement through continuous maintenance and reconstruction of hotel buildings and land materials. The expression 'the future is in history' reflects a historicizing process that includes earlier generations' farming activities. The Åkerblads and Tällbergsgården hotel business activities are linked to these 'activity pasts' (Schatzki, 2010, p. 102) in connection to which we can imagine a range of meanings expressed by members belonging to a 22-generation family.

Our understanding and interpretation of activities referred to in the five stories highlight existential space and bodily lived place.

THERE IS SPACE *AND* PLACE

As pointed out, in addition to *space* there is *place* where people become inhabitants through bodily placilizing (Casey, 2001), yet not place-bound since place is always under construction, unfolding paths in present open-endedness to a past and a future (Ingold, 2011). People find themselves in business activities, inherently temporal extending as materials become utilized in ways that enable existential space, and walked and muscularly engaged with in relation to place, making salient the bodily lived. Business activities are not performed *in* space or *located* to a specific place since business activities *are* temporality and movement (cf. Schatzki, 2010). Yet, movement does not exclude rest.

There is rest in terms of 'at-homeness' as Seamon (1985, pp. 227–9) expresses it, 'grounded in an atmosphere of care and concern for places, things, and people'. As Jerk Åkerblad insists: 'Tällbergsgården does not define a job or a company but a home and a way of life.' Harald Alm refers to home in terms of comfort and 'links between things and things and between things and people'. In the Klockargården story we listen to the words of Kerstin Sanfridson as she relates to Tällberg as her home, and to her nephew Anders Sandberg conveying Tällberg as 'a place where you feel at home', and Tällberg as 'coming home'. At-homeness involves also strong emotional attachments (Seamon, 2018) as reflected by a child's longingness for home comfort as indicated by Signe Alm.

The Tällberg place does not present itself as a spatial area that merely serves as a location for the five hotels referred to in the stories, or as a context that situates and embeds or surrounds the hotels. Not confined within a Tällberg area or context, people entwine with business activities, proceeding along paths threaded by people not living any longer, connecting with them while also celebrating newness and drawing new paths and resting.

By considering that place as landscape emerges as condensations of activity (Ingold, 2011) the focus shifts to activities woven into place, and place woven into activities. Under the names of Siljanstrand, Siljansgården, Green Hotel, Klockargården and Åkerblads-Tällbergsgården pieces of the Tällberg scaped land are made visible through present future-oriented human activities that re-actualize activities of a past.

ADDING TO EXISTING FAMILY BUSINESS RESEARCH

'Since Aristotle's claim that knowledge is derived from the understanding of the whole and not that of the single part (Aristotle's Holism), researchers have been struggling with systems and parts in terms of their contents and their relative dynamics', acknowledge Mele et al. (2010, p. 126). Family business research mirrors Aristotle's claim and has also an affinity for Parsons' (1951 [1970]) open systems theory. Open systems theory 'looks at the relationships between the organizations and the environment in which they are involved ... The organization is seen as a system built by energetic input-output where the energy coming from the output reactivates the system' (Mele et al., 2010, p. 127). The family business system consists of interactions between at least two systems; the family and the business (Nordqvist et al., 2015). Family and business constitute a whole, entitized with boundaries drawn around to discern the internal from the external. The family firm context refers to 'the unique opportunities, challenges, and resulting behavior and performance implications arising from residing at the intersection of the family system and the business system' (Madison et al., 2017b, p. 46).

The notion of context has been discussed in terms of a dynamic process 'embedded in a system's intrinsic operational "situatedness"' (Bate, 2014, p. 11), and a becoming ontology has been applied to show how process thinking helps in tracking and understanding changes in all subsystems of the family firm (Rondi, 2015). Yet, existing family business research seems to favour a systems view that draws a distinction between the internal and the external (e.g. Kammerlander et al., 2015; McCollom, 1992; Pieper & Klein, 2007; Rautiainen et al., 2012; Sharma & Salvato, 2013; Whetten et al., 2014; Zellweger & Nason, 2008) with the co-evolvement of the family and the business systems regarded as a 'truly realistic' approach (Neubauer, 2003, p. 269), 'Theory and practice indicate that in family-influenced firms, the interaction of the family unit, the business entity, and individual family members create unique systemic conditions and constituencies that impact the performance outcomes of the family business social system', assert Habbershon et al. (2003, p. 451). There is also a tendency in business history studies of family businesses to differentiate between the internal and the external. Long-term survival and longevity are dependent on the adaptability of the family business to changing internal and external conditions. From the viewpoint of Hoy (2014) the history of the family business should include external and internal factors and show how they lead to the survival and success of the family business.

As pointed out in the book (Chapter 2), research on family business commonly focuses on a family-business-system context and on what goes on inside of this context. Considerable attention is given to the social with little notion of the spatial material. The topic of succession gains a salient position but the serviceability, conduciveness and usability of materials for the extension of activities, and material imprints made as paths are trailed by predecessors, attract little interest. The social is highlighted with regard paid to knowledge, entrepreneurial orientation, emotions and the human relational. Studies present the location of the family business and describe the context as an external environment in which the family business is situated and embedded or surrounded by, largely disregarding space and place material.

Admittedly, there is a spatial bounding of family business, a presumed systems context as something present-at-hand available for a study. 'If we let go of the bounding in space and time the implication becomes that we retract from the organization as a pre-existing entity and turn towards studying organization as an emergent phenomenon', remarks Hernes (2004, p. 8). From a hermeneutic-phenomenological perspective family business dissolves into activities with which people entwine in amongst materials. Family business loses its systems context character, and 'environment' becomes a question of circumspective concern and closeness as described by a readiness-to-hand. In Heidegger's (1962, p. 135, emphasis in original) words: 'What is ready-to-hand in our everyday dealings has the character of *closeness* ... and what is close in this way gets established by circumspection of concern.' As Mugerauer (1985, p. 57) contends, 'environment is neither a brute given to be recorded passively in seemingly objective, scientific language nor a raw material to be organized according to coherent cultural patterns by an actively creative'. Instead, we seek what Heidegger (1962) calls the 'worldhood' of the environment, which refers to entities we encounter as being close to us and circumspectively interpreted. Deprived of worldhood the environment is rather a spatial context given in advance of extended things that are present-at-hand. For beings-in-the-world there are involvements of entities not merely present-at-hand but also ready-to-hand. The spatiality 'where' question thus directs us to things that manifest themselves in a readiness-to-hand, effectuated as tools (or equipment) when practically used. People reside in and dwell alongside the world. Environment is given 'proximally as that which becomes known' (Heidegger, 1962, p. 87) not merely confronted in perception and judgement but in care, conditioned by affective mood as a matter of concern.

Family-business-system-*as*-context and *within*-context descriptions (Chapter 2) neglect a mode of being in the world that accounts for 'worldhood' elicited in terms of circumspective concern and closeness. A study that advances a hermeneutic-phenomenological understanding of the social in relation to the material in connection to existential space and bodily lived place shifts the focus away from entitized conceptions of context to 'entity' in the constitution of *entity-ness*, accountable for *existence* and *being* (Heidegger, 1962). Entity in its entity-ness shows itself in a flow of activities, constituted of human interactions and relations. Its being nature implicates an ontological relationship with the world, meaning that the world comes not afterword but beforehand. As Relph (1985, p. 17) explains, 'we do not specifically occupy ourselves with the world, for it is so self-evident and so much a matter of course and we are so implicated in it that we are usually quite oblivious to it'. We are thrown into a world that we share with others and cannot escape from until all our future possibilities are closed down and we move towards death (Heidegger, 1962). The world then is not a system that consists of subsystems subjected to examination from the 'outside'.

Family business research has been dominated by quantitative methods (Nordqvist et al., 2009). Notwithstanding the usefulness and value of these methods, it is pertinent to note that there is a need for interpretive and critical studies. Nordqvist et al. (2009, p. 302) argue for an interpretative approach that 'has an ambition to conceptualize and contribute with new theory through novel, sometimes critical interpretations.' Qualitative studies are well suited to developing theory, 'designed to answer questions that begin with "how" or "why"', add Reay and Zhang (2014, p. 574). Critical implies 'imagining and explaining extraordinary alternatives, being sceptical about knowledge and solutions that present the only truth', submits Fletcher (2014, p. 151). Highlighting the need to add to existing family business research a spatial-material dimension that prompts us to pay attention to 'family business' *as activities* with a concern for the hermeneutic-phenomenological notion that we are storytelling beings-in-the-world, the book proposes an alternative approach, a theory of socio-material weaving implied in which is a narrative truth.

DEVELOPMENT OF THEORY IN QUALITATIVE RESEARCH

While the development of theory has been consistently associated with systematic observation, evidence, explanation, validation and generalization there is lack of consensus on what theory is (Sutton & Staw, 1995). Most social scientists embrace theory as 'covering laws' (DiMaggio, 1995), a scientific description that attempts to explain a phenomenon in a way that can be tested and corrected (Stewart et al., 2010). The researcher considers it possible to present evidence on the basis of complete and accurate analyses, building theory through activities such as induction, deduction and abduction to ensure scientific treatment (Dooley, 2002).

Torraco (2002) discusses inductive theory building in connection to case study research and grounded theory. A case study aims at a complete understanding of a phenomenon in its real-world context (Eisenhardt, 1989; Yin, 1989), 'not by controlling variables but rather by observing all of the variables and their interacting relationships', emphasizes Dooley (2002, p. 336). Described in this way, case study reflects positivistic thinking (Czarniawska, 1997), building on a source of evidence that supposedly separates the individual from the world. Grounded theory

(Glaser & Strauss, 1967) too assumes a split between individual and world, imitating quantitative ideals for collecting, coding and analysing data (Alvesson, 2003). Evidence is accumulated by the researcher on the basis of concepts and hypotheses that emerge from data, comparisons of data sorted into categories, and analyses of relationships between central categories (Egan, 2002). As I have pointed out elsewhere (Ericson, 2007), inductive theorizing tends to unbind and separate out experience to reach conclusions (Bacon, 1620 [2004]), assuming a Cartesian split between the individual and the world (Descartes, 1637 [1968]). Induction fails to recognize how one conceives of phenomena under investigation (Gadamer, 1989). The development of a socio-material weaving theory is informed by the philosophical tradition of hermeneutic philosophy, advancing the idea that we are beings-in-the-world with others and with materials, subverting dualistic conceptions of individual and world, actor and activity. Understanding, the explicit form of interpretation, is emphasized as something we undergo in interactions with one another, implicating that there is no evidence to be accumulated.

Deduction is based on the assumption that knowledge is created to explain and predict. Theories are first constructed and facts are then generated to be tested with resulting theories evaluated in terms of predictive success. Gold et al. (2011, p. 236) define abduction as the production of hypotheses 'in the form of empirical generalizations about individual objects', arguing that neither induction nor deduction is enough for building theory. Abduction includes detection of an empirical phenomenon and the exploration of 'potential explanatory patterns within facts of a phenomenon' (Åsvoll, 2014, p. 291). 'Phenomena exist to be explained rather than serve as the objects of prediction in theory testing', comments Haig (2005, p. 371). The explanatory theories generated are systematically re-evaluated against rival theories. For the building of a socio-material weaving theory, explanatory patterns within 'facts' of a phenomenon are not of central concern.

To induction, deduction and abduction theory building activities can be added meta-analytic and social constructionist theorizing (Torraco, 2002). Meta-analytic theorizing aims at synthesizing and organizing existing empirical findings by means of statistical techniques into a coherent pattern. Social constructionist theory development occurs on the basis of the sense that people make of the social world in their everyday lives. It is concerned with explanations of how social experience is created and given meaning, seeking 'increased powers of perception and understanding as an end in itself, whether it is rooted in interpretive, explanatory, or emancipatory objectives', says Torraco (2002, p. 362). With Fletcher (2006) we should note, though, that there is a variety of definitional emphases and applications of social construction with roots in intellectual traditions such as symbolic interaction with its focus on subjective meaning (Blumer, 1969; Mead, 1932), social phenomenology with attention directed to conscious experience originating in social interaction (Schutz, 1967) and cultural psychology with interest paid to relations and coordination between people and context (Gergen, 1999).

Social construction, a concept launched by Berger and Luckmann (1967), refers to the way in which people through negotiations and shared understandings construct reality, yet many social constructionist scholars are more concerned with individuals' subjective experiences than their engagement in social processes, notes Fletcher (2006). Those using constructionism interchangeably with constructivism tend to follow Vygotsky (1981) and Bruner (1990) with a focus on individuals' cognitive processes and the social and cultural mediation of these processes. A variant of constructionism called 'relational constructionism' gives 'more emphasis to individuals as "relational beings", who, in relations to past and future interactions/relations engage in acts of becoming' (Fletcher, 2006, p. 427). Akin to hermeneutic-phenomenological inspired theorizing, social relational constructionist theory development moves us beyond determinist understandings of social behaviour, practice and agency, yet with little interest devoted to existential spatial ways in which relational beings engage materials with their doings.

Qualitative researchers develop theories from a wide range of philosophical perspectives and there is no 'right way' for theory development. Referring to Kuhn's (1962 [1996]) interest in paradigms and how paradigms condition and shape the development of theories, Stewart et al. (2010, p. 227) hold that there is no single way of defining theory and developing theory; theories are 'outcomes of social processes as much as so-called scientific investigation'. Theory is not only about covering laws and could even be tentative. From the perspective of DiMaggio (1995) we should admit hybrid theories, combining qualities developed through the use of different theorizing approaches. DiMaggio (1995) presents theory as enlightenment, which is often intuitive and makes room for paradox without requiring conceptual clarity, and theory as a narrative view that includes empirical tests of the plausibility of the narrative. Pentland (1999) adopts the theory as narrative view, purporting that narrative data can provide a useful source for the development of process theory. Drawing concepts and analogies from narrative theory, he conceptualizes process as a set of interacting roles and subplots, taking into account a surface level and deeper structural levels. When analysing narrative 'we are starting with raw material that is central to the cognitive and cultural world of our subjects', explains Pentland (1999, p. 717). The underlying narrative structures are stories, used to explain the surface text structure for the development of theory.

Also in this book stories are of crucial importance for the development of theory but they are not used as 'raw material', derived from subjects separated from a world. The being-in-the-world narrative methodology (Chapter 4) does not separate the individual from the world. The individual is pre-narratively engaged with the world (Ricoeur, 1992). 'We author our lives. We narrate our lives' (Roth, 2018, p. 746).

A Theory of Socio-Material Weaving

A theory of socio-material weaving develops via insights gained from family business and socio-material organization and management studies (Chapters 2 and 3). Drawing inspiration from geographical and anthropological studies that engage hermeneutic-phenomenological work a clear distinction is made between space and place. The theory brings existential space and bodily lived place to the fore, ontologically embracing a hermeneutic-phenomenological being-in-the-world view, conjoined with *Dasein* that foregrounds our entwinement with activity – in amongst materials. The suggested theory moves beyond an understanding of space and place as objectivist contexts and subjectivist cognitive and affective contexts (cf. Seamon, 2018).

The theory of socio-material weaving directs attention to activities, constituted of the sociality of human interactions and relations, interwoven with the material. 'Weaving' (Chapter 4) is an activity that brings the social and the material together such as material is appropriated in activity, engaged *with* activity. The theory approaches the material as things that can function as tools (or equipment), depending on circumstances attributed theoretical and practical significance with a move from theoretical to practical significance implying a changed way of immersing in activities and the enabling of existential space. Differences in material significance reflect differences in a human's way of being. Some aspects of material might be competing and as a result, tension develops between theoretical and practical significance. Incompatible use of materials prompts revisiting theoretical significance (Lamprou, 2017).

The theory of socio-material weaving is thus concerned with the way in which material comes to matter in activity and is ascribed serviceability, conduciveness and usability for the extension of activities (Heidegger, 1962). It presupposes a being nature of material things, transcending the objectness of material and material agent and the abstractness of materiality, presuming that in care, conditioned by affective mood, the human circumspectively interprets the use of materials, the readiness-to-hand of which is a matter of circumspective concern. Affective mood, which denotes a person's sensitivity to, responsiveness to and reflection of emerging circumstances (Schatzki, 2010), mobilizes action that helps extend business activities through the use of material, creating a space that is existential in character (cf. Lamprou, 2017). Action 'is *what* happens in the happening that is activity' as Schatzki (2010, p. xv, emphasis in original) clarifies (Chapter 3). Activity, inherently temporal, does not occur 'in time'.

In addition to 'space' there is 'place', experientially explored (cf. Lefebvre, 1991). Geography and anthropology studies, drawing on hermeneutic-phenomenological work, break up the totemic conception of space and place (cf. Hubbard & Kitchin, 2010). Place is presented with reference to the bodily lived. The theory of socio-material weaving borrows from Casey (2001) the concepts of tenacity and subjection, concerned with our experience of place and the way in which place becomes part of us through placilizing the body, and from Ingold (2011) the concept of landscape is borrowed to bring to the fore paths threaded by inhabitants. The suffix 'scape' means 'to shape' and makes us aware of paths (or lines) trailed by people with their bodies and sometimes with the help of domestic animals (Ingold, 2011).

A FINAL COMMENT

In the hermeneutic-phenomenological ontological light of being-in-the-world (Heidegger, 1962), a pre-scientific pre-narrative relationship between the individual and the world (Ricoeur, 1992), the book makes a suggestion for an alternative approach that translates into a theory of socio-material weaving, reflecting a critical stance towards systems-oriented descriptions of family business. Complementing existing family business research it emphasizes flows of business activities, constituted of human interactions and relations, interwoven with materials. Tentative in character the theory aims for plausibility, implied in which is a narrative truth.

A narrative truth takes precedence over a logic that accentuates validation and universal application on the basis of tested models and cause–effect relationships (cf. Bruner, 1990). A narrative truth implies sensitivity to the storytellers' words and provides a theory of 'good reason'. A good theory is a plausible theory (Weick, 1989) and rich in points (Alvesson & Sköldberg, 2009) it adds something new, in the combination of concepts enabling understanding and making sense of a phenomenon along new lines, accounting for imagination and usefulness (Corley & Gioia, 2011; DiMaggio, 1995).

The book only scratches the surface of the social and the material, space and place, and mentions some material things that mainly relate to buildings and land. So a lot of work still remains for the 'goodness' of a theory of socio-material weaving. Hopefully, the book can inspire such an attempt. There is a need for philosophical-theoretical-empirical studies that provide more detailed elaboration on the dimensions of social and material, space and place, and contribute with richer stories of activities immersed in materials, carefully describe materials, reflect on how care conditioned by affective mood relates to feelings and emotions, how various materials are appropriated in activity, how webs of significances are constructed and existential space is promoted or inhibited.

In a world where technological innovations and space-planning connections make place obsolete (Agnew, 2011) and we communicate and interact in cyberspace it is all the more important in future research of the social and the spatial material to also complement studies of space with studies of place, differentiating between space and place, elevating place in terms of a world of materials lived and explored by the human body. The sensuousness of our flesh 'shocks us into remembering the fundamental activity of the human body: to feel the world' (Grange, 1985, p. 72). Place in its material bodily lived extension implies a continuous *taking in* (Seamon, 2018); the 'enactive vehicle of being-in-place is the *body*' (Casey, 2001, p. 687, emphasis in original).

In addition to existential space there is place, under the name of Tällberg, of a shifting blue with white weft threads going through materials that relate us to the sky, earth and water (cf. Forslund, 1922). Far from interconnected digital technology extending through a space that has no horizon, in the words of Heidegger (1971, p. 149): 'Earth is the serving bearer, blossoming and fruiting, spreading in rock and water, rising up into plant and animal ... The sky is the vaulting path of the sun, the course of the changing moon, the wandering glitter of the stars ...'

References

Adiguna, R. (2015). Organizational culture and the family business. In M. Nordqvist, L. Melin, M. Waldkirch & G. Kumeto (eds), *Theoretical Perspectives on Family Businesses* (pp. 156–74). Cheltenham, UK and Northampton, MA, USA: Edward Elgar Publishing.

Agnew, J.A. (2011). Space and place. In J.A. Agnew & D.N. Livingstone (eds), *The SAGE Handbook of Geographical Knowledge* (pp. 316–30). London: Sage.

Ahlström Söderling, R. (2019). *Flickebarnet Signe*. Lund, Sverige: Videpro.

Ahlund, T. (1994). *Om Klockare i Torsång*. Retrieved 6 October 2020 from https://docplayer.se/200482979-Om-klockare-i-torsang-av-thorild-ahlund.html

Åkerblad, C. (2008). *Historien om en gård i Tällbergs by. Gatugården i Tällberg från 1400-talet till dagens moderna Åkerblads hotell och Gästgiveri. Del I.* Falun, Sverige: Intellecta.

Åkerblad, C. (2009). *Historien om en gård i Tällbergs by. Gatugården i Tällberg från 1400-talet till dagens moderna Åkerblads hotell och Gästgiveri. Del II.* Falun, Sverige: Intellecta.

Åkerblads Website (2020). Retrieved 6 October 2020 from https://akerblads.se/

Akhter, N. (2016). *Family Business Portfolios: Enduring Entrepreneurship and Exit Strategies*. Jönköping, Sweden: Jönköping International Business School.

Akhter, N. (2015). Kinship and the family business. In M. Nordqvist, L. Melin, M. Waldkirch & G. Kumeto (eds), *Theoretical Perspectives on Family Businesses* (pp. 175–90). Cheltenham, UK and Northampton, MA, USA: Edward Elgar Publishing.

Akhter, N., Brundin, E., & Härtel, C. (2016). Transgenerational moral emotions: activating compassion to develop a positive organization. In N. Akhter (Dissertation). *Family Business Portfolios; Enduring Entrepreneurship and Exit Strategies* (pp. 189–230). Jönköping, Sweden: Jönköping International Business School.

Aksu- Koç, A., & Aktan-Erciyes, A. (2018). Narrative discourse: developmental perspectives. In A. Bar-On & D. Ravid (eds), *Handbook of Communications Disorders. Theoretical, Empirical, and Applied Linguistic Perspectives* (pp. 329–56). Amsterdam: De Gruyter Mouton.

Allouche, J., Amann, B., Jaussaud, J., & Kurashina, T. (2008). The impact of family control on the performance and financial characteristics of family versus nonfamily businesses in Japan: a matched-pair investigation. *Family Business Review, 21*(4), 315–30.

Alm, H. (1969). *Kärlek på jorden. Siljansgården och Siljanskolan under Femtio år. Minnen, Tankar, Drömmar.* Falun, Sverige: Seelig.

Almeida, P., & Kogut, B. (1999). Localization of knowledge and the mobility of engineers in regional networks. *Management Science*, *45*(7), 905–17.

Alvesson, M. (2003). Beyond neopositivists, romantics, and localists: a reflexive approach to interviews in organizational research. *Academy of Management Review*, *28*(1), 13–33.

Alvesson, M., & Kärreman, D. (2007). Constructing mystery: empirical matters in theory development. *Academy of Management Review*, *32*(4), 1265–81.

Alvesson, M., & Sköldberg, K. (2009). *Reflexive Methodology. New Vistas for Qualitative Research*. London: Sage.

Astrachan, J.H., & Shanker, M.C. (2003). Family businesses' contribution to the U.S. economy: a closer look. *Family Business Review*, *16*(3), 211–19.

Astrachan, J.H., Klein, S.B., & Smyrnios, K.X. (2002). The F-PEC scale: a proposal for solving the *family business* definition problem 1. *Family Business Review*, *15*(1), 45–58.

Astrachan, J.H., Pieper, T.M., & Jaskiewicz, P. (2008). *Family Business*. Cheltenham, UK and Northampton, MA, USA: Edward Elgar Publishing.

Åsvoll, H. (2014). Abduction, deduction and induction: can these concepts be used for an understanding of methodological processes in interpretive case studies? *International Journal of Qualitative Studies in Education*, *27*(3), 289–307.

Au, K., Craig, J.B., & Ramachandran, K. (2011). *Family Entrepreneurship in Asia Pacific: Exploring Transgenerational Entrepreneurship in Family Firms*. Cheltenham, UK and Northampton, MA, USA: Edward Elgar Publishing.

Aylett, R., & Louchart, S. (2003). Towards a narrative theory of virtual reality. *Virtual Reality*, *7*(1), 2–9.

Bachelard, G. (1992). *The Poetics of Space*. Boston, MA: Beacon Press.

Bacon, F. (1620). *The Instauratio Magna*. Reprinted in G. Rees & M. Weakly (eds), (2004). *The Oxford Francis Bacon*. Oxford: Clarendon Press.

Bakhtin, M.M. (1981). *The Dialogical Imagination. Four Essays*. Austin, TX: University of Texas Press.

Balogun, J., Jacobs, C.D., Jarzabkowski, P., Mantere, S., & Vaara, E. (2014). Placing strategy discourse in context: sociomateriality, sensemaking, and power. *Journal of Management Studies*, *51*(2), 175–201.

Barad, K. (2003). Posthumanist performativity: toward an understanding of how matter comes to matter. *Signs*, *28*(3), 801–31.

Barad, K. (2007). *Meeting the Universe Halfway*. Durham, NC: Duke University Press.

Barthes, R., & Duisit, L. (1975). An introduction to the structural analysis of narrative. *New Literary History*, *6*(2), 237–72.

Basco, R. (2015). Family business and regional development – a theoretical model of regional familiness. *Journal of Family Business Strategy*, *6*(4), 259–71.

Basco, R., Calabrò, A., & Campopiano, G. (2019). Transgenerational entrepreneurship around the world: implications for family business research and practice. *Journal of Family Business Strategy*, *10*(4), 1–16.

Bate, P. (2014). *Perspectives on context*. The Health Foundation. Retrieved 2 May 2019 from https://www.health.org.uk/sites/default/files/PerspectivesOn ContextBateContextIsEverything.pdf

Baù, M., Hellerstedt, K., Nordqvist, M., & Wennberg, K.J. (2013). Succession in family firms. In R.L. Sorenson, A. Yu, K.H. Brigham & G.T. Lumpkin (eds), *The Landscape of Family Business* (pp. 167–97). Cheltenham, UK and Northampton, MA, USA: Edward Elgar Publishing.

Beech, N., & Johnson, P. (2005). Discourses of disrupted identities in the practice of strategic change. The mayor, the street-fighter and the insider-out. *Journal of Organizational Change Management, 18*(1), 31–47.

Bellas, J. (2006). Interface between organisational design and architectural. In S.R. Clegg & M. Kornberger (eds), *Space, Organization and Management Theory* (pp. 241–7). Copenhagen: CBS Press.

Bengtson, V.L., & Allen, K.R. (1993). The life course perspective applied to families over time. In P. Boss, W.J. Doherty, R. LaRossa, W.R. Schumm & S.K. Steinmetz (eds), *Sourcebook of Family Theories and Methods. A Contextual Approach* (pp. 469–504). New York: Springer.

Berg, P.O., & Kreiner, K. (1990). Corporate architecture. Turning physical settings into symbolic resources. In P. Gagliardi (ed.), *Symbols and Artifacts: Views of the Corporate Landscape* (pp. 41–65). New York: Aldine de Gruyter.

Berger, P.L., & Luckmann, T. (1967). *The Social Construction of Reality*. London: Penguin.

Berghoff, H. (2006). The end of family business? The Mittelstand and German capitalism in transition, 1949–2000. *Business History Review, 80*(2), 263–95.

Berghoff, H. (2013). Blending personal and managerial capitalism: Bertelsmann's rise from medium-sized publisher to global media corporation and service provider, 1950–2010. *Business History, 55*(6), 855–74.

Berrone, P., Cruz, C., & Gomez-Mejia, L.R. (2012). Socioemotional wealth in family firms: theoretical dimensions, assessment approaches, and agenda for future research. *Family Business Review, 25*(3), 258–79.

Bika, Z., Rosa, P., & Karakas, F. (2019). Multilayered socialization processes in transgenerational family firms. *Family Business Review, 32*(3), 233–58.

Binder, T., & Hellström, M. (eds) (2005). *Design Spaces*. Helsinki: Edita.

Bjuggren, P-O., & Sund, L-G. (2001). Strategic decision-making in intergenerational successions of small- and medium-size family-owned businesses. *Family Business Review, 14*(1), 11–23.

Björnberg, Å., & Nicholson, N. (2012). Emotional ownership: the next generation's relationship with the family firm. *Family Business Review, 25*(4), 374–90.

Blombäck, A., & Craig, J. (2014). Marketing from a family business perspective. In L. Melin, M. Nordqvist & P. Sharma (eds), *The SAGE Handbook of Family Business* (pp. 423–41). London: Sage.

Blumer, H. (1969). *Symbolic Interactionism*. Englewood Cliffs, NJ: Prentice Hall.

Boje, D.M. (1991). The storytelling organization: a study of story performance. *Administrative Science Quarterly, 36*(1), 106–28.

Boje, D.M. (2000). *Narrative Methods for Organizational and Communication Research*. New York: Sage.

Boje, D.M., Luhman, J.T., & Baack, D.E. (1999). Stories and encounters between storytelling organizations. *Journal of Management Inquiry*, *8*(4), 340–60.

Botero, I., & Betancourt, G.G. (2016). Governing structures and family firms and their use in Latin America. In F.W. Kellermanns & F. Hoy (eds), *Routledge Companion to Family Business* (pp. 549–66). New York: Routledge.

Bourdieu, P. (1977). *Outline of a Theory of Practice*. Cambridge: Cambridge University Press.

Bozec, Y., & Di Vito, J. (2019). Founder-controlled firms and R&D investments: new evidence from Canada. *Family Business Review*, *32*(1), 76–96.

Brigham, K.H., & Payne, G.T. (2019). Socioemotional wealth (SEW): questions on construct validity. *Family Business Review*, *32*(4), 326–9.

Brown, A.D., & Rhodes, C. (2005). Narrative, organizations and research. *International Journal of Management Reviews*, *7*(3), 167–88.

Brundin, E., & Sharma, P. (2012). Love, hate, and desire: the role of emotional messiness in the business family. In A. Carsrud & M. Brännback (eds), *Understanding Family Business* (pp. 55–71). New York: Springer-Verlag.

Bruner, J. (1990). *Acts of Meaning*. Cambridge, MA: Harvard University Press.

Börjeson, H.E. (1974). *Fullbokat. Om charterflygets första tjugo år och om ett hotell i Tällberg*. Stockholm: Properius.

Cadieux, L., Lorrain, J., & Hugron, P. (2002). Succession in women-owned family businesses: a case study. *Family Business Review*, *15*(1), 17–30.

Çalişkan, K., & Callon, M. (2010). Economization, part 2: a research programme for the study of markets. *Economy and Society*, *39*(1), 1–32.

Cambridge English Dictionary (2020). Retrieved 10 January 2020 from https://dictionary.cambridge.org/dictionary/english/village

Cappelli, P., & Scherer, P.D. (1991). The missing role of context in OB: the need for a meso-level approach. *Research in Organizational Behavior*, *13*, 55–110.

Carbrea-Suárez, K., De Saá-Pérez, P., & García-Almeida, D. (2001). The succession process from a resource and knowledge-based view of the family firm. *Family Business Review*, *14*(1), 37–46.

Carbrea-Suárez, M.K., García-Almeida, D.J., & De Saá-Pérez, P. (2018). A dynamic network model of the successor's knowledge construction from the resource- and knowledge-based view of the family firm. *Family Business Review*, *31*(2), 178–97.

Carlsson, T. (2018). *Stor hotellaffär i Tällberg*. Retrieved 28 February 2021 from https://www.siljannews.se/ekonomi/stor-hotellaffar-tallberg/

Carr, J.C., & Sequira, M.J. (2007). Prior family business exposure as intergenerational influence and entrepreneurial intent: a theory of planned behavior approach. *Journal of Business Research*, *60*(10), 1090–8.

Carroll, G., & Wade, J. (1991). Density dependence in the organizational evolution of the American brewing industry across different levels of analysis. *Social Science Research*, *20*(3), 271–302.

Casey, E.S. (1993). *Getting Back Into Place. Toward a Renewed Understanding of the Place-World*. Bloomington, IN: Indiana University Press.

Casey, E.S. (2001). Between geography and philosophy: what does it mean to be in the place-world? *Annals of the Association of American Geographers*, *91*(4), 683–93.

Cecez-Kecmanovic, D., Galliers, R.D., Henfridsson, O., Newell, S., & Vidgren, R. (2014). The sociomateriality of information systems: current status – future directions. *MIS Quarterly*, *38*(3), 809–30.

Chandler, A.D. (1962). *Strategy and Structure: Chapters in the History of the Industrial Enterprise*. Cambridge, MA: MIT Press.

Chandler, A.D. (1977). *The Visible Hand*. Cambridge, MA: Harvard University Press.

Chanlat, J-F. (2006). Space, organization and management thinking: a socio-historical perspective. In S.R. Clegg & M. Kornberger (eds), *Space, Organization and Management Theory* (pp. 17–43). Copenhagen: CBS Press.

Chapman, C.S., Chua, W.F., & Mahama, H. (2015). Actor-network theory and strategy as practice. In D. Golsorkhi, L. Rouleau, D. Seidl & E. Vaara (eds), *Cambridge Handbook of Strategy as Practice* (pp. 265–80). Cambridge: Cambridge University Press.

Chau, T.T. (1991). Approaches to succession in East Asian business organizations. *Family Business Review*, *4*(2), 161–79.

Chia, R. (2004). Strategy-as-practice: reflections on the research agenda. *European Management Review*, *1*(1), 29–34.

Chia, R., & Holt, R. (2006). Strategy as practical coping: a Heideggerian perspective. *Organization Studies*, *27*(5), 635–55.

Chia, R., & Rasche, A. (2015). Epistemological alternatives for researching strategy as practice: building and dwelling worldviews. In D. Golsorkhi, L. Rouleau, D. Seidl & E. Vaara (eds), *Cambridge Handbook of Strategy as Practice* (pp. 44–57). Cambridge: Cambridge University Press.

Chirico, F., & Salvato, C. (2016). Knowledge internalization and product development in family firms: when relational and affective factors matter. *Entrepreneurship Theory and Practice*, *40*(1), 201–29.

Chittoor, R., & Das, R. (2007). Professionalization of management and succession performance – a vital linkage. *Family Business Review*, *20*(1), 65–79.

Chrisman, J., Chua, J.H., & Litz, R.A. (2004). Comparing the agency costs of family and non-family firms: conceptual issues and exploratory evidence. *Entrepreneurship Theory and Practice*, *28*(4), 335–54.

Ciborra, C. (2006). The mind or the heart? It depends on (the definition of) situation. *Journal of Information Technology*, *21*(3), 129–39.

Clegg, S.R., & Kornberger, M. (eds) (2006). *Space, Organization and Management Theory*. Copenhagen: CBS Press.

Clegg, S.R., & Kornberger, M. (2015). Analytical frameworks for studying power in strategy as practice and beyond. In D. Golsorkhi, L. Rouleau, D. Seidl & E.Vaara (eds), *Cambridge Handbook of Strategy as Practice* (pp. 389–404). Cambridge: Cambridge University Press.

Colli, A. (2003). *History of Family Business, 1850–2000*. Cambridge: Cambridge University Press.

Colli, A., & Fernández Pérez, P. (2014). Business history and family firms. In L. Melin, M. Nordqvist & P. Sharma (eds), *The SAGE Handbook of Family Business* (pp. 269–92). London: Sage.

Colli, A., & Rose, M. (2008). Family business. In G.G. Jones & J. Zeitlin (eds), *The Oxford Handbook of Business History* (pp. 194–218). New York: Oxford University Press.

Cooren, F., Bencherki, N., Chaput, M., & Vásquez, C. (2015). The communicative constitution of strategy-making: exploring fleeting moments of strategy. In D. Golsorkhi, L. Rouleau, D. Seidl & E. Vaara (eds), *Cambridge Handbook of Strategy as Practice* (pp. 365–88). Cambridge: Cambridge University Press.

Corley, K.G., & Gioia, D.A. (2011). Building theory about theory building: what constitutes a theoretical contribution? *Academy of Management Review, 36*(1), 12–32.

Countryside Hotels Website (2021). Retrieved 25 November 2020 from https://www.countrysidehotels.se/en/about-us/

Cropanzano, R., & Mitchell, M. (2005). Social exchange theory: an interdisciplinary review. *Journal of Management, 31*(6), 874–900.

Cruz, C., & Nordqvist, M. (2012). Entrepreneurial orientation in family firm: a generational perspective. *Small Business Economics, 38*(1), 33–49.

Cunliffe, A.L. (2002). Social poetics as management inquiry: a dialogical approach. *Journal of Management Inquiry, 11*(2), 128–45.

Cunliffe, A.L, Luhman, J.T., & Boje, D.M. (2004). Narrative temporality: implications for organizational research. *Organization Studies, 25*(2), 261–86.

Czarniawska, B. (1997). *Narrating the Organization.* Chicago, IL: University of Chicago Press.

Czarniawska, B. (2004). *Narratives in Social Science Research.* London: Sage.

D'Adderio, L. (2011). Artifacts at the centre of routines: performing the material turn in routines theory. *Journal of Institutional Economics, 7*(2), 197–230.

Dalarna (2016). *Arkeologi i Dalarna.* Årgång 86. Dalarna, Sverige: Dalarnas Forminnes och Hembygdsförbund.

Dalarnas Tidningar (2015). Retrieved 20 January 2020 from https://www.dt.se/artikel/35-ar-sedan-tagolyckan-mellan-hinsnoret-och-ornas

Dale, K., & Burrell, G. (2008). *The Spaces of Organization and the Organization of Space. Power, Identity and Materiality at Work.* New York: Palgrave Macmillan.

Dale, K., & Burrell, G. (2010). 'All together, altogether better': the ideal of 'community' in the spatial reorganization of the workplace. In A. Van Marrewijk & D. Yanow (eds), *Organizational Spaces. Rematerializing the Workaday World* (pp. 19–40). Cheltenham, UK and Northampton, MA, USA: Edward Elgar Publishing.

Dameron, S., Lê, J.K., & LeBaron, C. (2015). Materializing strategy and strategizing materials: why matter matters. *British Journal of Management, 26*(S1), S1–S12.

Daspit, J.J., Holt, D.T., Chrisman, J.J., & Long, R.G. (2016). Examining family firm succession from a social exchange perspective: a multiphase, multistakeholder review. *Family Business Review, 29*(1), 44–64.

Davis, J.A., Pitts, E.L., & Cormier, K. (2000). Challenges facing family companies in the Gulf region. *Family Business Review, 13*(3), 217–38.

Davis, J.H., Shoorman, F.D., & Donaldson, L. (1997). Toward a stewardship theory of management. *The Academy of Management Review, 22*(1), 20–47.

Dawson, A., & Hjorth, D. (2011). Advancing family business research through narrative analysis. *Family Business Review, 25*(3), 339–55.

De Fina, A. (2009). Narratives in interview – the case of accounts. For an interactional approach to narrative genres. *Narrative Inquiry, 19*(2), 233–58.

De La Ville, V-I., & Mounoud, E. (2015). A narrative approach to strategy as practice: strategy-making from texts and narratives. In D. Golsorkhi, L. Rouleau, D. Seidl & E. Vaara (eds), *Cambridge Handbook of Strategy as Practice* (pp. 249–64). Cambridge: Cambridge University Press.

De Massis, A., Sharma, P., Chua, J.H., & Chrisman, J.J. (2012). *Family Business Studies. An Annotated Bibliography*. Cheltenham, UK and Northampton, MA, USA: Edward Elgar Publishing.

De Massis, A., Seger, P., Chua, J.H., & Vismara, S. (2016). Incumbents' attitude toward intrafamily succession: an investigation of its antecedents. *Family Business Review, 29*(3), 278–300.

Debicki, B.J., Kellermanns, F.W., Chrisman, J.J., Pearson, A.W., & Spencer, B.A. (2016). Development of socio-emotional wealth importance (SEW) scale for family research. *Journal of Family Business Strategy, 7*(1), 47–57.

Dejung, C. (2013). Worldwide ties: the role of family business in global trade in the nineteenth and twentieth centuries. *Business History, 55*(6), 1001–18.

Deleuze, G., & Guattari, F. (2004). *A Thousand Plateaus: Capitalism and Schizophrenia*. London: Continuum.

Descartes, R. (1637). *Discourse on Method and the Meditations*. Reprinted in 1968. London: Penguin Books.

Dibrell, C., Bettinelli, C., & Randerson, C. (2017). Market orientation and innovativeness in family firms: the moderating influence of organizational social consciousness. In F.W. Kellermanns & F. Hoy (eds), *The Routledge Companion to Family Business* (pp. 267–80). New York and London: Routledge.

Dickstein, S. (2004). Material attachment and family functioning: use of narrative methodology. In M.W. Pratt & B.H. Fiese (eds), *Family Stories and the Life Course: Across Time and Generations* (pp. 213–34). Hillsdale, NJ: Lawrence Erlbaum.

DiMaggio, P.J. (1995). Comments on 'What theory is not'. *Administrative Science Quarterly, 40*(3), 391–7.

Discua Cruz, A., Hamilton, E., &. Jack, S. (2012). Understanding entrepreneurial cultures in family businesses: a study of family entrepreneurial teams in Honduras. *Journal of Family Business Strategy, 3*(3), 147–61.

Donckels, R., & Fröhlich, E. (1991). Are family businesses really different? European experiences from STRATOS. *Family Business Review, 4*(2), 149–60.

Dooley, L.M. (2002). Case study research and theory building. *Advances in Developing Human Resources, 4*(3), 335–54.

Egan, T.M. (2002). Grounded theory research and theory building. *Advances in Developing Human Resources, 4*(3), 277–95.

Eisenhardt, K.M. (1989). Building theory from case study research. *The Academy of Management Review, 14*(4), 532–50.

Elpidorou, A., & Freeman, L. (2015). Affectivity in Heidegger I: moods and emotions in *Being and Time*. *Philosophy Compass, 10*(10), 661–71.

Erdogan, I., Rondi, E., & De Massis, A. (2020). Managing the innovation and the tradition paradox in family firms: a family imprinting perspective. *Entrepreneurship Theory and Practice, 44*(1), 20–54.

Ericson, M. (2007). *Business Growth: Activities, Themes and Voices*. Cheltenham, UK and Northampton, MA, USA: Edward Elgar Publishing.

Ericson, M. (2010). *A Narrative Approach to Business Growth*. Cheltenham, UK and Northampton, MA, USA: Edward Elgar Publishing.

Ericson, M. (2014). On the dynamics of fluidity and open-endedness of strategy process toward a strategy-as-practicing conceptualization. *Scandinavian Journal of Management, 30*(1), 1–15.

Ericson, M. (2018). *Moral Human Agency. A Missing Dimension in Strategy as Practice*. Cambridge: Cambridge University Press.

Ericson, M., & Kjellander, B. (2018). The temporal becoming self. Towards a *Ricoeurian* conceptualization of identity. *Scandinavian Journal of Management, 34*(2), 205–14.

Ericson, M., & Melin, L. (2010). Strategizing and history. In D. Golsorkhi, L. Rouleau, D. Seidl & E. Vaara (eds), *Cambridge Handbook of Strategy as Practice* (pp. 326–43). Cambridge: Cambridge University Press.

Escobar, M. (2018). *The Guestroom of the Future: Hyper-personalized, Hyper-connected*. Retrieved 16 June 2021 from https://hospitalitytech.com/guestroom-future-hyper-personalized-hyper-connected

Etymology Dictionary (2020). Retrieved 4 April 2019 from https://www.etymonline.com/word/context

Evert, R.E., Martin, J.A., McLeod, M.S., & Payne, G.T. (2016). Empirics in family business research: progress, challenges, and the path ahead. *Family Business Review, 29*(1), 17–43.

Fiese, B.H., & Pratt, M.W. (2004). Conclusions and future directions. In M.W. Pratt & B.H. Fiese (eds), *Family Stories and the Life Course: Across Time and Generations* (pp. 401–18). Hillsdale, NJ: Lawrence Erlbaum.

Fisher, W.R. (1984). Narration as a human communication paradigm: the case of public moral argument. *Communication Monographs, 51*(1), 1–22.

Fivush, R., Bohanek, J., Robertson, R., & Duke, M. (2004). Family narratives and the development if children's emotional well-being. In M.W. Pratt & B.H. Fiese (eds), *Family Stories and the Life Course: Across Time and Generations* (pp. 55–76). Hillsdale, NJ: Lawrence Erlbaum.

Fletcher, D. (2006). Entrepreneurial processes and the social construction of opportunity. *Entrepreneurship and Regional Development, 18*(5), 421–40.

Fletcher, D. (2007). Toy Story: the narrative world of entrepreneurship and the creation of interpretive communities. *Journal of Business Venturing, 22*(5), 649–72.

Fletcher, D. (2014). Family business inquiry as a critical social science. In L. Melin, M. Nordqvist & P. Sharma (eds), *The SAGE Handbook of Family Business* (pp. 137–54). London: Sage.

Fletcher, D., Melin, L., & Gimeno, A. (2012). Culture and values in family business – a review and suggestions for future research. *Journal of Family Business Strategy*, 3(3), 127–31.

Forslund, K-E. (1922). *Med Dalälven från källorna till havet*. Del 1. Österdalälven, bok IX. (I Tällberg). Leksandsboken,Stockholm: Åhlén & Åkerlund.

Frykman, H. (2010). *Siljansgården i Tällberg*. Retrieved 5 September 2019 from http://blogg.bergmanolson.se/?p=400

Frödin, J. (1925). *The Fäbod-District around Lake Siljan. Publications of the New Society of Letters at Lund.* Lund, Sweden: C.W.K. Gleerup.

Gadamer, H-G. (1989). *Truth and Method.* New York: Continuum.

Gagliardi, P. (ed.) (1990). *Symbols and Artifacts: Views of the Corporate Landscape.* New York: Aldine de Gruyter.

García-Alvarez, E., & Lòpez-Sintas, J. (2001). A taxonomy of founders based on values: the root of family business heterogeneity. *Family Business Review*, 4(3), 209–30.

Gergen, K.J. (1999). *An Invitation to Social Construction.* Los Angeles, CA: Sage.

Gergen, K.J., & Gergen, M.M. (1997). Narratives of the self. In L.P. Hinchman & S.K. Hinchman (eds), *Memory, Identity, Community. The Idea of Narrative in the Human Science* (pp. 161–84). New York: State University of New York Press.

Gersick, K.E., Davis, J.A., McCollom Hampton, M., & Lansberg, I. (1997). *Generation to Generation: Life Cycles in Family Business.* Cambridge, MA: Harvard University Press.

Gherardi, S. (2017). Sociomateriality in posthumanist practice theory. In A. Hui, T. Schatzki & E. Shove (eds), *The Nexus of Practices: Connections, Constellations, Practitioners* (pp. 38–51). London: Routledge.

Gibbs, P. (2008). What is work? A Heideggerian insight into work as a site for learning. *Journal of Education and Work*, 21(5), 423–34.

Giménez, E.L., & Novo, J.A. (2020). A theory of succession in family firms. *Journal of Family and Economic Issues*, 41, 96–120.

Gimeno Sandig, A., Labadie, G.J., Saris, W., & Mayordomo, X.M. (2006). Internal factors of family business performance: an integrated theoretical model. In P.Z. Poutziouris, K.X. Smyrnios & S.B. Klein (eds), *Handbook of Research of Family Business* (pp. 145–64). Cheltenham, UK and Northampton, MA, USA: Edward Elgar Publishing.

Ginalski, S. (2013). Can families resist managerial and financial revolutions? Swiss family firms in the twentieth century. *Business History*, 55(6), 981–1000.

Glaser, B.G., & Strauss, A.L. (1967). *The Discovery of Grounded Theory. Strategies for Qualitative Research.* New Brunswick, NJ: Aldine.

Goel, S., Jussila, I., & Ikäheimonen, T. (2014). Governance in family firms: a review and research agenda. In L. Melin, M. Nordqvist & P. Sharma (eds), *The SAGE Handbook of Family Business* (pp. 226–48). London: Sage.

Gold, J., Walton, J., Cureton, P., & Anderson, L. (2011). Theorising and practitioners in HRD: the role of abductive reasoning. *Journal of European Industrial Training, 35*(3), 230–46.

Gomez-Mejia, L.R., Haynes, K.T., Núñez-Nickel, M., Jacobson, K.J.L., & Moyano-Fuentes, J. (2007). Socio-emotional wealth and business risks in family-controlled firms: evidence from Spanish olive oil mills. *Administrative Science Quarterly, 52*(2), 106–37.

Graburn, N.H.H. (2001). What is tradition? *Museum Anthropology, 24*(2/3), 6–11.

Grafström, M., & Lid Falkman, L. (2017). Everyday narratives: CEO rhetoric on twitter. *Journal of Organizational Change Management, 30*(3), 312–22.

Grange, J. (1985). Place, body and situation. In D. Seamon & R. Mugerauer (eds), *Dwelling, Place and Environment. Towards a Phenomenology of Person and World* (pp. 71–84). New York: Columbia University Press.

Green Hotel Website (2019). Retrieved 1 July 2019 from https://www.greenhotel.se/sv/om-oss

Green Hotel Website (2020). Retrieved 16 January 2020 from https://www.greenhotel.se/sv/om-oss

Greve, H. (2000). Market niche entry decisions: competition, learning and strategy in Tokyo banking, 1894–1936. *Academy of Management Journal, 43*(5), 816–36.

Gupta, V., Levenburg, N.M., Moore, L.L., Motwani, J., & Schwarz, T. (2011). The spirit of family business: a comparative analysis of Anglo, Germanic and Nordic nations. *International Journal of Cross Cultural Management, 11*(2), 133–51.

Haag, K. (2012). *Rethinking Family Business Succession: From a Problem to Solve to an Ongoing Practice.* Jönköping, Sweden: Jönköping International Business School.

Haag, K., Helin, J., & Melin, L. (2006). *Practices of communication in the strategic context of succession.* Paper presented at the EGOS Colloquium in Bergen, Norway.

Habbershon, T.G., & Williams, M.L. (1999). A resource-based framework for assessing the strategic advantages of family firms. *Family Business Review, 12*(1), 1–25.

Habbershon, T.G., Williams, M., & MacMillan, I. (2003). A unified systems perspective of family firm performance. *Journal of Business Venturing, 18*(4), 451–65.

Haig, B.D. (2005). An abductive theory of scientific method. *Psychological Methods, 10*(4), 371–88.

Hall, A. (2003). *Strategising in the Context of Genuine Relations.* Jönköping, Sweden: Jönköping International Business School.

Hall, A., & Nordqvist, M. (2008). Professional management in family businesses: toward an extended understanding. *Family Business Review, 21*(1), 51–69.

Hall, A., Melin, L., & Nordqvist, M. (2001). Entrepreneurship as radical change in the family business: exploring the role of cultural patterns. *Family Business Review, 14*(3), 193–208.

Hamilton, E. (2006). Narratives of enterprise as epic tragedy. *Management Decision, 44*(4), 536–50.

Hamilton, E., Discua Cruz, A., & Jack, S. (2017). Reframing the status of narrative in family business research: towards an understanding of families in business. *Journal of Family Business Strategy, 8*(1), 3–12.

Handler, W.C. (1994). Succession in family businesses: a review of the research. *Family Business Review, 7*(2), 133–57.

Harman, G. (2016). Agential and speculative realism: remarks on Barad's ontology. *Rhizomes: Cultural Studies in Emerging Knowledge, 30*, 1–7.

Harrison, M-C. (2014). Reading the marriage plot. *Journal of Family Theory and Review, 6*(1), 112–31.

Hatch, M.J. (1990). The symbolic of office design. An empirical exploration. In P. Gagliardi (ed.), *Symbols and Artifacts: Views of the Corporate Landscape* (pp. 129–44). New York: Aldine de Gruyter.

Heidegger, M. (1962). *Being and Time*. New York: Harper & Row.

Heidegger, M. (1971). Building, dwelling, thinking. In A. Hofsdater (ed.), *Poetry, Language and Thought* (pp. 143–62). New York: Harper & Row.

Helin, J. (2011). *Living Moments in Family Meetings. A Process Study in the Family Business Context*. Jönköping, Sweden: Jönköping International Business School.

Helin, J., & Jabri, M. (2015). Family business succession in dialogue: the case of differing backgrounds and views. *International Small Business Journal, 34*(4), 487–505.

Herlihy, D. (1991). Family. *The American Historical Review, 96*(1), 1–16.

Hernes, T. (2004). *The Spatial Construction of Organization*. Amsterdam: John Benjamin.

Hernes, T., Bakken, T., & Olsen, P.I. (2006). Spaces as process: developing a recursive perspective on organizational space. In S.R. Clegg & M. Kornberger (eds), *Space, Organization and Management Theory* (pp. 44–63). Copenhagen: CBS Press.

Herrero, I. (2018). How familial is family social capital? Analyzing bonding social capital in family and nonfamily firms. *Family Business Review, 31*(4), 441–59.

Hjorth, D. (2005). Organizational entrepreneurship with Michel de Certeau on creating heterotopias (or spaces of play). *Journal of Management Inquiry, 14*(4), 386–98.

Hodges, H. (1976). *Artefacts: An Introduction to Early Materials and Technology*. London: John Baker.

Holt, R., & Popp, P. (2013). Emotion, succession, and the family firm: Josiah Wedgwood & Sons. *Business History, 55*(6), 892–909.

Holy, L. (1996). *Anthropological Perspectives on Kinship*. London: Pluto.

Hoy, F. (2014). Entrepreneurial venturing for family business research. In L. Melin, M. Nordqvist & P. Sharma (eds), *The SAGE Handbook of Family Business* (pp. 620–8). London: Sage.

Hubbard, P., & Kitchin, R. (2010). *Key Thinkers on Space and Place*. London: Sage.

Hutton, J. (2018). *Aristotle's Poetics*. New York: W.W. Norton & Company.

Hyvärinen, M. (2010). Revisiting the narrative turns. *Life Writing*, *7*(1), 29–82.

Hällberg, A. (2006). *Hundan, vilken hotellsvit!* Retrieved 28 February 2020 from https://www.dt.se/artikel/hundan-vilken-hotellsvit

Ibrahim, A.B., Soufani, K., & Lam, J. (2001). A study of succession in a family firm. *Family Business Review*, *14*(3), 245–58.

Iedema, R., Long, D., & Carroll, K. (2010). Corridor communication, spatial design and patient safety: enacting and managing complexities. In A. Van Marrewijk & D. Yanow (eds), *Organizational Spaces. Rematerializing the Workaday World* (pp. 41–57). Cheltenham, UK and Northampton, MA, USA: Edward Elgar Publishing.

Ingels, M. (2017). *Hotell i Tällberg går samman.* Retrieved 5 September 2019 from https://www.siljannews.se/leksand/hotell-tallberg-gar-samman/

Ingold, T. (1993). The temporality of the landscape. *World Archaeology*, *25*(2), 152–74.

Ingold, T. (2011). *Being Alive. Essays of Movement, Knowledge and Description.* New York: Routledge.

Introna, L.D. (2013). Otherness and the letting-be of becoming: or ethics beyond bifurcation. In P.R. Carlile, D. Nicolini, A. Langley & H. Tsoukas (eds), *How Matter Matters: Objects, Artifacts, and Materiality in Organization Studies* (pp. 260–87). Oxford: Oxford University Press.

Jaffe, D.T., & Lane, S.H. (2004). Sustaining a family dynasty: key issues facing complex multigenerational business- and investment-owning families. *Family Business Review*, *17*(1), 81–98.

James, H. (2006). *Family Capitalism, Wendels, Haniels, Falcks, and the Continental European Model.* Cambridge, MA: Harvard University Press.

Jarzabkowski, P., & Kaplan, S. (2015). Strategy tools-in-use: a framework for understanding 'technologies for rationality' in practice. *Strategic Management Journal*, *36*(4), 537–58.

Jaskiewicz, P., Combs, J.G., & Rau, S.B. (2015). Entrepreneurial legacy: toward a theory of how some family firms nurture transgenerational entrepreneurship. *Journal of Business Venturing*, *30*(1), 29–49.

Jennings, J.E., Breitkreuz, R.S., & James, A.E. (2014). Theories from family science: a review and roadmap for family business research. In L. Melin, M. Nordqvist & P. Sharma (eds), *The SAGE Handbook of Family Business* (pp. 25–46). London: Sage.

Jennings, J.E., Eddleston, K.A., Jennings, P.D., & Sarathy, R. (eds) (2015). *Firms Within Families: Enterprising in Diverse Country Contexts*, Cheltenham, UK and Northampton, MA, USA: Edward Elgar Publishing.

Johns, G. (2006). The essential impact on organizational behaviour. *The Academy of Management Review*, *31*(2), 386–408.

Jones, G., & Rose, M.B. (1993). Family capitalism. *Business History*, *35*(4), 1–16.

Jones, G., & Zeitlin, J. (eds) (2008). *The Oxford Handbook of Business History.* New York: Oxford University Press.

Kammerlander, N., & Holt, D.T. (2018). Introductory comment on 'the succession process from a resource and knowledge-based view of the family firm'. *Family Business Review*, *31*(2), 176–7.

Kammerlander, N., Sieger, P., Voordeckers, W., & Zellweger, T.M. (2015). Value creation in family firms: a model of fit. *Journal of Family Business Strategy*, *6*(2), 63–72.

Kaplan, S. (2011). Strategy and power point: an inquiry into the epistemic culture and machinery of strategy making. *Organization Science*, *22*(2), 320–46.

Kar, S.K., & Samantarai, M. (2011). Narrative research on 'Bothra': an Indian family firm. *Society and Business Review*, *6*(2), 131–48.

Kenis, P., Kruyen, P.M., & Basijens, J.M.J. (2010). Bendable bars in a Dutch prison: a creative place in a non-creative space. In A. Van Marrewijk & D. Yanow (eds), *Organizational Spaces. Rematerializing the Workaday World* (pp. 58–76). Cheltenham, UK and Northampton, MA, USA: Edward Elgar Publishing.

Klein, S.B. (2000). Family businesses in Germany: significance and structure. *Family Business Review*, *13*(3), 157–81.

Klein, S.B., Astrachan, J.H., & Smyrnios, K.X. (2005). The F-PEC scale of family influence: construction, validation, and further implication for theory. *Entrepreneurship Theory & Practice*, *29*(3), 321–39.

Klockargården (2020). *Hotell Hantverk & Nöjen*. Brochure.

Klockargården History (2020). *Klockargården exhibition.*Tällberg, Dalarna.

Klockargården Website (2018). Retrieved 20 July from https://www.klockargarden.com/sv

Klockarås, C. (2010). *Storaffär i Tällberg*. christer.klockaras@dt.se

Kornberger, M., & Clegg, S.R. (2004). Bringing space back in: organizing the generative building. *Organization Studies*, *25*(7), 1095–114.

Kuhn, T.S. (1962). *The Structure of Scientific Revolutions*. Reprinted in 1996. Chicago, IL: University of Chicago Press.

Kumeto, G. (2015). Behavioural agency theory and the family business. In M. Nordqvist, L. Melin, M. Waldkirch & G. Kumeto (eds), *Theoretical Perspectives on Family Businesses* (pp. 78–98). Cheltenham, UK and Northampton, MA, USA: Edward Elgar Publishing.

Kurbits (2021). Retrieved 28 February 2021 from https://sonesgarden.se/Kult_ide_hist/Kurbits/Kurbits.html

Labaki, R., Michael-Tsabari, N., & Zachary, R.K. (2013). Emotional dimensions within the family business: towards a conceptualization. In K.X. Smyrnios, P.Z. Poutziouris & S. Goel (eds), *Handbook of Research on Family Business* (pp. 734–63). Cheltenham, UK and Northampton, MA, USA: Edward Elgar Publishing.

Lamprou, E. (2017). Spatiality as care: a Heideggerian perspective on sociomaterial practices. *Organization Studies*, *38*(2), 1733–52.

Lansberg, I.S. (1983). Managing human resources in family firms: the problem of institutional overlap. *Organizational Dynamics*, *12*(1), 39–46.

Latour, B. (1987). *Science in Action: How to Follow Scientists and Engineers through Society*. Cambridge, MA: Harvard University Press.

Latour, B. (2005). *Reassembling the Social: An Introduction to Actor-Network-Theory*. Oxford: Oxford University Press.

Law, J., & Mol, A. (1995). Notes on materiality and sociality. *The Sociological Review*, *43*(2), 274–94.

Lê, J., & Spee, P. (2015). The role of materiality in the practice of strategy. In D. Golsorkhi, L. Rouleau, D. Seidl & E. Vaara (eds), *Cambridge Handbook of Strategy as Practice* (pp. 582–97). Cambridge: Cambridge University Press.

Le Breton-Miller, I., & Miller, D. (2009). Agency vs. stewardship in public family firms: a social embeddness reconciliation. *Entrepreneurship Theory and Practice, 33*(6), 1169–91.

Le Breton-Miller, I., & Miller, D. (2018). Looking back at and forward from: 'family governance and firm performance: agency, stewardship, and capabilities'. *Family Business Review, 31*(2), 229–37.

Le Breton-Miller, I., Miller, D., & Steier, L.P. (2014). Toward an integrative model of effective FOB succession. *Entrepreneurship Theory and Practice, 28*(4), 305–28.

Lefebvre, H. (1991). *The Production of Space*. Oxford: Blackwell.

Leonardi, P.M. (2011). When flexible routines meet flexible technologies: affordance, constraint, and the imbrications of human and material agencies. *MIS Quarterly, 35*(1), 147–67.

Les Hénokiens (2020). Retrieved 19 February 2020 from https://www.henokiens.com/content

Liljas, J.M. (2016). 'En ny musikuppfostran': reformpedagogiska anspråk i Siljanskolans bildningsinnehåll. *Nordic Journal of Educational History, 3*(1), 47–74.

Lindgren, H. (2002). *Succession strategies in a large family business group: the case of the Swedish Wallenberg family*. Paper prepared for the 6th European Business History Association Annual Congress in Helsinki, Finland.

Lindqvist, A. (2020). *Märtha Fredrique Grahn, Svensk Kvinnobiografiskt Lexikon*. Retrieved 28 February 2021 from https://skbl.se/sv/artikel/MarthaFredriqueGahn

Lussier, R.N., & Sonfield, M.C. (2012). Family businesses' succession planning: a seven-country comparison. *Journal of Small Business and Enterprise Development, 19*(1), 7–19.

MacIntyre, A. (1981). *After Virtue. A Study of Moral Theory*. London: Bloomsbury.

Madison, K., Kellermanns, F.W., & Munyon, T.P. (2017a). Coexisting agency and stewardship governance in family firms: an empirical investigation of individual-level and firm-level effects. *Family Business Review, 30*(4), 347–68.

Madison, K., Li, Z., & Holt, D.T (2017b). Agency theory in family firm research: accomplishments and opportunities. In F.W. Kellermanns & F. Hoy (eds), *The Routledge Companion to Family Business* (pp. 45–69). New York and London: Routledge.

Martinez, M.A., & Aldrich, H. (2014). Sociological theories applied to family business. In L. Melin, M. Nordqvist & P. Sharma (eds), *The SAGE Handbook of Family Business* (pp. 83–99). London: Sage.

Mazzelli, A. (2015). Behavioural theory and the family business. In M. Nordqvist, L. Melin, M. Waldkirch & G. Kumeto (eds), *Theoretical Perspectives on Family Businesses* (pp. 35–57). Cheltenham, UK and Northampton, MA, USA: Edward Elgar Publishing.

McAdams, D.P. (2004). Generativity and the narrative ecology of family life. In M.W. Pratt & B.H. Fiese (eds), *Family Stories and the Life Course: Across Time and Generations* (pp. 235–58). Hillsdale, NJ: Lawrence Erlbaum.

McCollom, M. (1992). Organizational stories in a family-owned business. *Family Business Review*, 5(1), 3–24.

McMillan Lequieu, A. (2015). Keeping the farm in the family name: patrimonial narratives and negotiations among German-heritage farmers. *Rural Sociology*, 80(1), 39–59.

Mead, G.H. (1932). *The Philosophy of the Present*. Chicago, IL: University of Chicago Press.

Meier, O., & Schier, G. (2016). The early succession stage of a family firm: exploring the role of agency rationales and stewardship attitudes. *Family Business Review*, 29(3), 256–77.

Mele, C., Pels, J., & Polese, F. (2010). A brief review of systems theories and their managerial applications. *Service Science*, 2(1/2), 126–35.

Melin, L., Nordqvist, M., & Sharma, P. (eds) (2014). *The SAGE Handbook of Family Business*. London: Sage.

Miller, D., & Le Breton-Miller, I. (2006). Family governance and firm performance: agency, stewardship, and capabilities. *Family Business Review*, 19(1), 73–87.

Miller, D., Wiklund, J., & Yu, W. (2020). Mental health in the family business: a conceptual model and a research agenda. *Entrepreneurship Theory and Practice*, 44(1), 55–80.

Mobach, M. (2010). Virtual worlds for organizational spaces. In A. Van Marrewijk & D. Yanow (eds), *Organizational Spaces. Rematerializing the Workaday World* (pp. 159–73). Cheltenham, UK and Northampton, MA, USA: Edward Elgar Publishing.

Mugerauer, R. (1985). Language and the emergence of the environment. In D. Seamon & R. Mugerauer (eds), *Dwelling, Place and Environment* (pp. 51–70). New York: Columbia University Press.

Murphy, L., Huybrechts, J., & Lambrechts, F. (2019). The origins and development of socioemotional wealth within next-generation family members: an interpretive grounded theory study. *Family Business Review*, 32(4), 396–424.

Murray, B. (2003). The succession transition process: a longitudinal perspective. *Family Business Review*, 16(1), 17–33.

Måg, L-E. (2012). *Klockar Per skapar nytt Tällbergsboende*. Retrieved 5 September 2019 from https://www.dt.se/artikel/klockar-per-skapar-nytt -tallbergsboende

Müller, S., & Korsgaard, S. (2017). Resources and bridging the role of spatial context for entrepreneurship. *Entrepreneurship and Regional Development*, 30(1/2), 224–55.

Nadel, L., & Willner, J. (1980). Context and conditioning: a place for space. *Physiological Psychology*, 8(2), 218–28.

Naldi, L., Cennamo, C., Corbetta, G., & Gomez-Mejia, L. (2013). Preserving socioemotional wealth in family firm: asset of liability? The moderating role of business context. *Entrepreneurship Theory and Practice*, 37(6), 1341–60.

Neubauer, H. (2003). The dynamics of succession in family businesses in Western European countries. *Family Business Review, 16*(4), 269–81.

Neverman, L. (2020). *Root Cellars 101*. Retrieved 6 October 2020 from https://commonsensehome.com/root-cellars-101/

Nicholson, N. (2008). Evolutionary psychology and family business: a new synthesis for theory, research, and practice. *Family Business Review, 21*(1), 103–18.

Nicholson, N. (2014). Evolutionary theory: a new synthesis for family business thought and research. In L. Melin, M. Nordqvist & P. Sharma (eds), *The SAGE Handbook of Family Business* (pp. 119–36). London: Sage.

Nordqvist, M. (2005). *Understanding the Role of Ownership in Strategizing: A Study of Family Firms*. Jönköping, Sweden: Jönköping International Business School.

Nordqvist, M., Hall, A., & Melin, L. (2009). Qualitative research on family businesses: the relevance and usefulness of the interpretive approach. *Journal of Management & Organization, 15*(3), 294–308.

Nordqvist, M., Marzano, G., Brenes, E.R., Jiménez, G., & Fonseca-Paredes, M. (eds) (2011). *Understanding Entrepreneurial Family Business in Uncertain Environments: Opportunities and Resources in Latin America*. Cheltenham, UK and Northampton, MA, USA: Edward Elgar Publishing.

Nordqvist, M., Wennberg, K.J., Baù, M., & Hellerstedt, K. (2013). An entrepreneurial process perspective on succession in family firms. *Small Business Economics, 40*(4), 1087–122.

Nordqvist, M., Melin, L., Waldkirch, M., & Kumeto, G. (eds) (2015). *Theoretical Perspectives on Family Businesses*. Cheltenham, UK and Northampton, MA, USA: Edward Elgar Publishing.

Orlikowski, W.J. (2007). Sociomaterial practices: exploring technology at work. *Organization Studies, 28*(9), 1435–48.

Orlikowski, W.J. (2009). The sociomateriality of organizational life: considering technology in management research. *Cambridge Journal of Economics, 34*(1), 125–41.

Orlikowski, W.J., & Scott, S.V. (2008). Sociomateriality: challenging the separation of technology work and organization. *The Academy of Management Annals, 2*(1), 433–74.

Panayiotou, A., & Kafiris, K. (2010). Firms in film: representations of organizational space, gender and power. In A. Van Marrewijk & D. Yanow (eds), *Organizational Spaces. Rematerializing the Workaday World* (pp. 174–99). Cheltenham, UK and Northampton, MA, USA: Edward Elgar Publishing.

Pandit, N., & Cook, G. (2003). The benefits of industrial clustering: insights from the British financial services industry in three locations. *Journal of Financial Services Marketing, 7*(3), 230–45.

Parada, M.J., & Dawson, A. (2017). Building family business identity through transgenerational narratives. *Journal of Organizational Change Management, 30*(3), 344–56.

Parada, M.J., & Viládas, H. (2010). Narratives: a powerful device for values transmission in family businesses. *Journal of Organizational Change Management, 23*(2), 166–72.

Parsons, T. (1951). *The Social System.* Reprinted in 1970. Chatham, UK: Mackays of Chatham PLC.

Pearson, A.W., Carr, J.C., & Shaw, J.C. (2008). Toward a theory of familiness: a social capital perspective. *Entrepreneurship Theory and Practice, 32*(6), 949–69.

Peiser, R.B., & Wooten, L.M. (1983). Life cycle changes in small family businesses. *Business Horizons, 26*(3), 58–65.

Pentland, B.T. (1999). Building process theory with narrative: from description to explanation. *Academy of Management Review, 24*(4), 711–24.

Peterson, C., & McCabe, A. (2004). Echoing our parents: parental influences of children's narration. In M.W. Pratt & B.H. Fiese (eds), *Family Stories and the Life Course: Across Time and Generations* (pp. 27–54). Hillsdale, NJ: Lawrence Erlbaum.

Pieper, T., & Klein, S.B. (2007). The bulleye: a systems approach to modelling family firms. *Family Business Review, 20*(4), 301–19.

Pieper, T.M., Klein, S.B., & Jaskiewicz, P. (2008). The impact of goal alignment on board existence and top management team composition: evidence from family-influenced businesses. *Journal of Small Business Management, 46*(3), 372–94.

Polkinghorne, D.E. (1988). *Narrative Knowing and the Human Sciences.* New York: State University of New York Press.

Pratt, M.W., & Fiese, B.H. (2004). Family stories and the life course: an ecological context. In M.W. Pratt & B.H. Fiese (eds), *Family Stories and the Life Course: Across Time and Generations* (pp. 1–24). Hillsdale, NJ: Lawrence Erlbaum.

Press Release, 12 March 2018. *Buskowskis – där samlingarna säljs.* Retrieved 21 October 2019 from https://www.mynewsdesk.com/se/bukowskis/pressreleases

Proffitt Jr, W.T., & Zahn, G.L. (2006). Design, but align: the role of organisational physical space, architecture and design in communicating organisational legitimacy. In S.R. Clegg & M. Kornberger (eds), *Space, Organization and Management Theory* (pp. 204–20). Copenhagen: CBS Press.

Qualifications Cidesco (2021). Retrieved 14 January 2021 from https://estheticinstitute.com/cidesco/

Rae, D. (2005). Entrepreneurial learning: a narrative-based conceptual model. *Journal of Small Business and Enterprise Development, 12*(3), 323–35.

Rafali, A., & Pratt, M.G. (eds) (2006). *Artifacts and Organizations: Beyond Mere Symbolism.* Hillsdale, NJ: Lawrence Erlbaum.

Ramirez Pasillas, M., Brundin, E., & Markowska, M. (eds) (2017). *Contextualizing Entrepreneurship in Emerging Economies and Developing Countries.* Cheltenham, UK and Northampton, MA, USA: Edward Elgar Publishing.

Ratcliffe, M. (2013). Why mood matters. In M.A. Wrathall (ed.), *The Cambridge Companion to Heidegger's* Being and Time (pp. 157–76). New York: Cambridge University Press.

Rau, S.B. (2014). Resource-based view of family firms. In L. Melin, M. Nordqvist & P. Sharma (eds), *The SAGE Handbook of Family Business* (pp. 321–39). London: Sage.

Rautiainen, M., Pihkala, T., & Ikävalko, M. (2012). Family business systems models – a case study and some implications of open systems perspective. *Journal of Small Business & Entrepreneurship*, *25*(2), 155–68.

Reay, T., & Zhang, Z. (2014). Qualitative methods in family business research. In L. Melin, M. Nordqvist & P. Sharma (eds), *The SAGE Handbook of Family Business* (pp. 573–93). London: Sage.

Relph, E. (1985). Geographical experiences and being-in-the-world: the phenomenological origins of geography. In D. Seamon & R. Mugerauer (eds), *Dwelling, Place and Environment* (pp. 5–31). New York: Columbia University Press.

Richardson, B. (2000). Recent concepts of narrative and the narratives of narrative theory. *Style*, *34*(2), 168–75.

Ricoeur, P. (1984). *Time and Narrative*. Volume 3. Chicago, IL: University of Chicago Press.

Ricoeur, P. (1992). *Oneself as the Other*. Chicago, IL: University of Chicago Press.

Riessman, C.K. (1993). *Narrative Analysis*. Retrieved 16 June 2021 from https://core.ac.uk/download/pdf/58322.pdf

Ring, J.K., Brown, J., & Matherne, C.F. (2017). Family firms, stakeholders relationships, and competitive advantage. A review and directions for future research. In F.W. Kellermanns & F. Hoy (eds), *The Routledge Companion to Family Business* (pp. 159–74). New York and London: Routledge.

Rondi, E. (2015). Process thinking and the family business. In M. Nordqvist, L. Melin, M. Waldkirch & G. Kumeto (eds), *Theoretical Perspectives on Family Businesses* (pp. 119–36). Cheltenham, UK and Northampton, MA, USA: Edward Elgar Publishing.

Roth, B. (2018). Reading from the middle: Heidegger and the narrative self. *European Journal of Philosophy*, *26*(2), 746–62.

Rönnblad, M. (2010). *Folkfest I Tällberg*. Retrieved 1 September 2019 from http://www.dalademokraten.se/artikel/folkfest-i-tallberg-1

Sandberg, J., & Dall'Alba, G. (2009). Returning to practice anew: a life-world perspective. *Organization Studies*, *30*(12), 1349–68.

Sandberg, J., & Tsoukas, H. (2011). Grasping the logic of practice: theorizing through practical rationality. *Academy of Management Review*, *36*(2), 338–60.

Schatzki, T.R. (1996). *Social Practices. A Wittgenstein Approach to Human Activity and the Social*. New York: Cambridge University Press.

Schatzki, T.R. (2005). The sites of organizations. *Organization Studies*, *26*(3), 465–84.

Schatzki, T.R. (2010). *The Timespace of Human Activity: On Performance, Society, and History as Indeterminate Teleological Events*. Plymouth, UK: Lexington.

Schulze, W.S., Lubatkin, M.H., & Dino, R.N. (2003). Toward a theory of agency and altruism in family firms. *Journal of Business Venturing*, *18*(4), 473–90.

Schutz, A. (1967). *The Phenomenology of the Social World*. Evanston, IL: Northwestern University Press.

Seamon, D. (1985). Reconciling old and new worlds: the dwelling-journey relationship as portrayed in Vilhelm Moberg's 'Emigrant' novels. In D.

Seamon & R. Mugerauer (eds), *Dwelling, Place and Environment, Towards a Phenomenology of Person and World* (pp. 227–45). New York: Columbia University Press.

Seamon, D. (2018). *Life Takes Place – Phenomenology, Lifeworlds, and Place Making.* New York: Routledge.

Sharma, P., & Salvato, C. (2013). Family firm longevity: a balancing act between continuity and change. In P. Fernandez Perez & A. Colli (eds), *The Endurance of Family Businesses: A Global Overview* (pp. 34–56). New York: Cambridge University Press,

Shephard, D.A., & Suddaby, R. (2017). Theory building: a review and integration. *Journal of Management, 43*(1), 59–86.

Shotter, J. (2003). 'Real presences': meaning as living movement in a participatory world. *Theory & Psychology, 13*(4), 435–68.

Shotter, J. (2014). Agential realism, social constructionism, and our living relations to our surroundings: sensing similarities rather than seeing patterns. *Theory & Psychology, 24*(3), 305–25.

Siljanstrand Website (2018). Retrieved 12 April 2018 from https://www.hotellsiljanstrand.se

Siljanstrand Website (2019). Retrieved 1 July 2019 from https://www.hotellsiljanstrand.se

Siljanstrand Website (2021). Retrieved 17 January 2021 from https://www.hotellsiljanstrand.se

Simon, A., Marquès, P., Bikfalvi, A., & Dolors Muñoz, M. (2012). Exploring value differences across family firms: the influence of choosing and managing complexity. *Journal of Family Business Strategy, 3*(3), 132–46.

Sjögren, H. (2018). *Family Dynasties: The Evolution of Global Business in Scandinavia.* New York: Routledge.

Sjöstrand, S-E. (1997). *The Two Faces of Management: The Janus Factor.* London: International Thomson Business Press.

Sluyterman, K.E., & Winkelman, H.J.M. (1993). The Dutch firm confronted with Chandler's dynamics of industrial capitalism, 1890–1940. *Business History, 35*(4), 152–83.

Smith, R. (2018). Reading luminal and temporal relationality in the Baxter family 'public narrative'. *International Small Business Journal, 36*(1), 41–59.

Smith, S. (1993). Future and failure: the survival of family firms in eighteenth-century India. *Business History, 35*(4), 45–65.

Smyrnios, K.X., Poutziouris, P.Z., & Goel, S. (eds) (2014). *Handbook of Research on Family Business.* Cheltenham, UK and Northampton, MA, USA: Edward Elgar Publishing.

Soja, E. (1996). *Thirdspace: Journeys to Los Angeles and Other Real-and-Imagined Places.* Oxford: Blackwell.

Sorenson, O., & Audia, P.G. (2000). The social structure of entrepreneurial activity: geographic concentration of footwear production in the US, 1940–1989. *American Journal of Sociology, 106*(2), 424–62.

Sorenson, R.L. (2014). Values in family business. In L. Melin, M. Nordqvist & P. Sharma (eds), *The SAGE Handbook of Family Business* (pp. 463–79). London: Sage.

Sorenson, R.L., Yu, A., Brigham, K.H., & Lumpkin, G.T. (eds) (2015). *The Landscape of Family Business*. Cheltenham, UK and Northampton, MA, USA: Edward Elgar Publishing.

Spee, P.A., & Jarzabkowski, P. (2011). Strategic planning as communicative process. *Organization Studies, 32*(9), 1217–45.

Spence, D.P. (1982). *Narrative Truth and Historical Truth. Meaning and Interpretation in Psychoanalysis*. New York: Norton.

Staffansson Pauli, K. (2015). Gender theory and family business. In M. Nordqvist, L. Melin, M. Waldkirch & G. Kumeto (eds), *Theoretical Perspectives on Family Businesses* (pp. 191–210). Cheltenham, UK and Northampton, MA, USA: Edward Elgar Publishing.

Steier, L., & Muethel, M. (2014). Trust and family businesses. In L. Melin, M. Nordqvist & P. Sharma (eds), *The SAGE Handbook of Family Business* (pp. 498–513). London: Sage.

Stewart, J., Harte, V., & Sambrook, S. (2010). What is theory? *Journal of European Industrial Training, 35*(3), 221–29.

Stough, R., Welter, F., Block, J.H., & Wennberg, K.J. (2015). Family business and regional science: 'bridging the gap'. *Journal of Family Business Strategy, 6*(4), 208–18.

Strati, A. (1999). *Organization and Aesthetics*. London: Sage.

Susanto, A.B., & Susanto, P. (2013). *The Dragon Network: Inside Stories of the Most Successful Chinese Family Businesses*. Singapore: John Wiley & Sons.

Sutton, R.I., & Staw, B.M. (1995). What theory is not. *Administrative Science Quarterly, 40*(3), 371–84.

Szydlik, M. (2012). Generations: connections across the life course. *Advances in Life Course Research, 17*(3), 100–11.

Tagiuri, R., & Davis, J. (1996). Bivalent attributes of the family firm. *Family Business Review, 9*(2), 199–208.

Tapper, G. (2018). *Konstsamlaren säljer livsverk*. Retrieved 21 October 2019 from https://weekend.di.se/nyheter/konstsamlaren-saljer-livsverk-1

Taylor, S., & Spicer, A. (2007). Time for space: a narrative review of research on organizational spaces. *International Journal of Management Reviews, 9*(4), 325–46.

Tokarcyk, J., Hansen, E., Green, M., & Down, J. (2007). A resource-based view and market orientation theory examination of the role of 'familiness' in family business success. *Family Business Review, 20*(1), 17–31.

Torraco, R.J. (2002). Research methods for theory building in applied disciplines: a comparative analysis. *Advances in Developing Human Resources, 4*(3), 355–76.

Tsoukas, H. (2015). Making strategy: meta-theoretical insights from Heideggerian phenomenology. In D. Golsorkhi, L. Rouleau, D. Seidl & E. Vaara (eds), *Cambridge Handbook of Strategy as Practice* (pp. 58–77). Cambridge: Cambridge University Press.

Tällbergs Byalag (2007). *Tällberg från bondby till turistby*. Tällbergs byalag för Hembygdsgård (1986–2007). Orsa, Sverige: Orsatryck.

Vaara, E., Sorsa, V., & Pälli, P. (2010). On the force potential of strategy texts: a critical discourse analysis of a strategic plan and its power effects in a city organization. *Organization, 17*(6), 685–702.

Van den Berghe, L.A.A., & Carchon, S, (2003). Agency relations within the family business system: an exploratory approach. *Corporate Governance: An International Review, 11*(3), 171–9.

Van Marrewijk, A. (2010). The beauty and the best: the embodied experience of two corporate buildings. In A. Van Marrewijk & D. Yanow (eds), *Organizational Spaces. Rematerializing the Workaday World* (pp. 96–114). Cheltenham, UK and Northampton, MA, USA: Edward Elgar Publishing.

Van Marrewijk, A.H, & Yanow, D. (eds) (2010). *Organizational Spaces. Rematerializing the Workaday World.* Cheltenham, UK and Northampton, MA, USA: Edward Elgar Publishing.

Vygotsky, L.S. (1981). The genesis of higher mental function. In J.V. Wertsch (ed.), *The Concept of Activity in Soviet Psychology* (pp. 144–88). Armonk, NY: M.E. Sharpe.

Waldkirch, M. (2018). *From Professional Interactions to Relational Work.* Jönköping, Sweden: Jönköping International Business School.

Waldkirch, M., & Nordqvist, M. (2017). Finding benevolence in family firms: the case of stewardship theory. In F.W. Kellermanns & F. Hoy (eds), *The Routledge Companion to Family Business* (pp. 401–14). New York and London: Routledge.

Weick, K.E. (1989). Theory construction as disciplined imagination. *The Academy of Management Review, 14*(4), 516–31.

Weimann, R. (1973). French structuralism and literary history: some critiques and reconsiderations. *New Literary History, 4*(3), 437–69.

Welch, J. (1991). Family enterprises in the United Kingdom, the Federal Republic of Germany and Spain: a transnational comparison. *Family Business Review, 4*(2), 191–203.

Welter, F. (2011). Contextualizing entrepreneurship – conceptual challenges and ways forward. *Entrepreneurship Theory and Practice, 35*(1), 165–84.

Welter, F., Brush, C., & De Bruin, A. (2014). *The gendering of entrepreneurship context.* Working Paper, 01/14. Institut for Mittelstandsforschung Bonn.

Werle, F., & Seidl, D. (2015). The layered materiality of strategizing: epistemic objects and the interplay between material artefacts in the exploration of strategic topics. *British Journal of Management, 26*(S1), 567–89.

Whetten, D., Foreman, P., & Dyer, W.G. (2014). Organizational identity and family business. In L. Melin, M. Nordqvist & P. Sharma (eds), *The SAGE Handbook of Family Business* (pp. 480–97). London: Sage.

Wigren, C. (2003). *The Spirit of Gnosjö the Grand Narrative and Beyond.* Jönköping, Sweden: Jönköping International Business School.

Wåhlin, N. (2006). Transcultural encounters in cities: convergence without becoming coincident. In S.R. Clegg & M. Kornberger (eds), *Space, Organization and Management Theory* (pp. 266–86). Copenhagen: CBS Press.

Xi, J., Zhang, S., Jin, L., & Holloway, G. (2016). Family business research in China: a field in the light of traditional culture and transforming society. In

F.W. Kellermanns & F. Hoy (eds), *Routledge Companion to Family Business* (pp. 483–505). New York and London: Routledge.

Yanow, D. (1998). Space stories: studying museum buildings as organizational spaces while reflecting on interpretive methods and their narration. *Journal of Management Inquiry, 7*(3), 216–39.

Yin, R.K. (1989). *Case Study Research. Design and Methods.* Los Angeles, CA: Sage.

Yu, X., Stanley, L., Li, Y., Eddleston, K.A., & Kellermanns, F.W. (2020). The invisible hand of evolutionary psychology: the importance of kinship in first-generation family firms. *Entrepreneurship Theory and Practice, 44*(1), 134–57.

Zahra, S.A., & Sharma, P. (2004). Family business research: a strategic reflection. *Family Business Review, 17*(4), 331–46.

Zeitlin, J. (2008). The historical alternatives approach. In G.G. Jones & J. Zeitlin (eds), *The Oxford Handbook of Business History* (pp. 120–40). New York: Oxford University Press.

Zellweger, T. (2017). *Managing the Family Business. Theory and Practice.* Cheltenham, UK and Northampton, MA, USA: Edward Elgar Publishing.

Zellweger, T.M., & Nason, R.S. (2008). A stakeholder perspective on family firm performance. *Family Business Review, 21*(3), 203–16.

Zellweger, T.M., Eddleston, K.A., & Kellermanns, F.W. (2010). Exploring the concept of familiness: introducing family firm identity. *Journal of Family Business Strategy, 1*(1), 54–63.

Index